Carol Himsel Daly, D.V.M.

Maine Coon Cats

Everything about Purchase, Care, Nutrition,
Reproduction, Diseases, and Behavior

With 38 Color Photographs
Illustrations by Michele Earle-Bridges

BARRON'S

Dedication

This book is dedicated affectionately
To my husband, Richard, waiting anxiously.
Not for this book to be upon the shelf;
Instead he waits for a different wealth.
Our family grows again by one;
At last a small person to share the fun
(Instead of a kitten, thank goodness, not another)
Of dogs and cats, their frolics and antics
In our peaceable kingdom and bring joy to her parents.

© Copyright 1995 by Barron's Educational Series, Inc.

All inquiries should be addressed to
Barron's Educational Series, Inc.
250 Wireless Boulevard
Hauppauge, NY 11788

International Standard Book No. 0-8120-9038-1

Library of Congress Catalog Card No. 95-14958

Library of Congress Cataloging-in-Publication Data
Himsel Daly, Carol.
    Maine coon cats : everything about purchase, care, nutrition, reproduction, diseases, and behavior / Carol Himsel Daly ; drawings by Michele Earle-Bridges.
        p.   cm.—(A complete pet owner's manual)
    Includes bibliographical references (p. 108) and index.
    ISBN 0-8120-9038-1
    1. Maine coon cat. I. Title. II. Series.
SF449.M34H55   1995
636.8r3—dc20   95-14958
                                                      CIP

PRINTED IN HONG KONG

5678   9955   987654321

About the Author

After practicing for several years in northern California, Dr. Carol Himsel Daly currently resides with her husband, Richard, on the Connecticut shoreline, where she practices veterinary medicine and surgery for small companion animals. In addition, Dr. Himsel is a veterinary consultant and has written research and clinical articles for the scientific community. She is also the author of *Rats—A Complete Pet Owner's Manual* and *Caring for Your Sick Cat*, both published by Barron's. When she is not caring for other people's animals, Dr. Himsel spends her time caring for Willie, Neige, Cocoa, and Molly, and dabbles in the arts of photography and cooking.

Photo Credits

Mark McCullough: cover, inside front cover, pages 16, 17, 20, 21, 24, 25, inside back cover; Chanan Photography: pages 5, 8, 9, 65, 68; Donna Coss: pages 12, back cover; Don Himsel: pages 28, 32 top, 33, 36 bottom, 40 bottom, 41, 49, 64 top, 73; Judith E. Strom: pages 29, 36 top, 37; Susan Green: pages 32 bottom, 40 top, 48, 52, 57, 64 bottom, 69, 72, 77, 80; Larry and Vickie Fisher: pages 44, 45, 61; Barbara Augello: page 53.

Important Notes

When you handle cats, you may sometimes get scratched or bitten. If this happens, have a doctor treat the injuries immediately.

Make sure your cat receives all the necessary shots and wormings, otherwise serious danger to the animal and to human health may arise. A few diseases and parasites can be communicated to humans. If your cat shows any signs of illness, you should definitely consult a veterinarian. If you are worried about your own health, see your doctor and tell him or her that you have a cat.

Some people have allergic reactions to cat hair. If you think you might be allergic, ask your doctor before you get a cat.

It is possible for a cat to cause damage to someone else's property and even to cause accidents. For your own protection, you should make sure your insurance covers such eventualities, and you should definitely have liability insurance.

Contents

Acknowledgments

The author is grateful to the distinguished author, lecturer, and veterinarian Dr. Fredric Frye for his thoughtful and expert review of the manuscript. Warmest appreciation goes to Maine coon cat breeders Terry Handel, Temora's Patricia Ledoux, and Coonquest's Larry Fisher for generously giving their time and materials, and to Claddacoon's Mary Hanafin, who also welcomed the author to her cattery and shared her beautiful cats. Thank you to Michele Earle-Bridges for her illustrations, to photojournalist Don Himsel for his contribution, and to Richard Myers from Just for Pets, Manchester, New Hampshire, and Amerkat's Anne Marie Berger for making some of those possible.

Preface

With this book I hope to give the reader a sense of the marvelously winsome nature and intelligence of one of my most favorite cats. Oh it is true—as some would say that I never met a cat I couldn't like for one reason or another—there is something very special about this breed. They're very practical. Maine coon cats are fur-bearing packages of New England spirit. They are as sensible as a good warm coat and boots. In fact, it is my opinion that if L.L Bean sold cats, they'd sell Maine coon cats. As you learn more about this breed, it should take little effort to imagine a Maine coon of long ago keeping company with the farmer in the sap house each spring, ever vigilant for field mice.

I do hope that you read this book before deciding upon and acquiring your kitten. It contains valuable information about preparing for, selecting, and caring for your companion. This book is also a good starting place for those interested in showing Maine coon cats because it includes useful references and suggestions on getting to know breeders. Your comments, stories about your own cats and suggestions on how to make this text more useful to you are warmly welcome.

Carol Himsel Daly, D.V.M.

This brown mackerel and white cat shows off its bushy ringed tail.

Understanding Your Maine Coon Cat

Chris crouches, then leaps, landing silently on the countertop above. Deftly, using his paw, he opens the cupboard door where his people keep the paper plates on which his dinner is served, and with his teeth, he removes precisely one and places it on the counter. Then he waits.

Intelligent, playful, cuddly, and engaging are words often used to describe the Maine coon cat. Their striking features and substantial size attract your first attention, but it's their personality that is the hook. Maine coon cats have been described as the "dog lover's cat" because of their com-

Fanciful tales abound concerning the origins of the Maine coon cat. Some hold the raccoon to be a forebear, while others say the bobcat is an ancestor.

panionable temperament. Maine coon cats love people! They follow you about the house not only for companionship but also to see what amusing things you may be up to. This longing for companionship along with their physical characteristics that enable them to withstand harsh winters are what brought them from their early beginnings in New England to contemporary life.

Origins of the Maine Coon Cat

There are many myths surrounding the Maine coon cat, especially regarding its origins. The myths are probably a lot more interesting than the truth, so the myths endure. The Maine coon cat of today is America's original cat, that is, the Maine coon as known is descended directly from the cats that were around during the time that New England was first settled. But where did those cats come from?

The most chimeric belief of all is that the first Maine coon cat was derived from the mating of a raccoon and a wild feline. This myth springs from the idea that the Maine coon cat's large size and bushy ringed tail are characteristics acquired from its raccoon forefather. Zoologists know that this is a genetically impossible occurrence; raccoons and cats simply do not have the proper "chemistry," biologically speaking, for this phenomenon to ever take place. In a related story, some say that the Maine coon cat is a descendant of the mating of a feral domestic cat and the bobcat that once hunted widely over the New England countryside. Although this mating may be possible, unlike the raccoon story, it does leave one to wonder, "where does the tail come from?"

Another fanciful tale tells that Maine coon cats are a descendant of Angora cats belonging to Marie Antoinette that were shipped to America for safe-keeping during the French Revolution. Once here, they mated with the native feral felines to produce the Maine coon breed. The research for this story and related others has been intriguingly described in the book *That Yankee Cat* by Marilis Hornidge (see Books, page 108), and although it contains some elements of truth, it is probably more romantic than genuine.

The Practical Cat

There are some things about the ancestors of Maine coon cats that are known to be true. Living conditions were extremely harsh in New England when this country was first settled. Cold weather arrived early, as early as late summer in the North, and proceeded into severe winters with much snow. The spring rains and thaw brought mud and flooding. To build a life out of conviction and ideals, devise shelter from the elements, and obtain food from the land required courage, endurance, resourcefulness, and adaptability from the people and the livestock they brought with them.

Cats came too. In fact, cats came aboard ships even before permanent settlements were established. Cats were useful to seamen because they helped control the rat population aboard the ships and were good company. When the ships landed ashore, it is likely that cats went ashore too, and some were probably left behind. Today, several European breeds of cats bear resemblance to the Maine coon cat. One of these breeds is the Norwegian forest cat. Perhaps it was

their ancestors who traveled on ships to the New World and stayed behind.

These cats produced offspring but only the offspring that were adaptable and bearing certain physical characteristics could survive in the harsh New England climate and conditions. Such cats might have had a large and sturdy frame and could fluff up and stand menacingly, as a deterrent to predators like wolves and coyotes. They would have had an easily maintained, long shaggy hair coat for protection against the cold, with very little undercoat to mat. Big furry paws would function like snowshoes and furry ears would keep out the snow as well.

And so it is concluded that the Maine coon cat has descended or ascended from necessity. These New England cats were prized during the nineteenth century. Beautiful yet practical in appearance and resourceful in talents, these Yankee cats were excellent hunters. Their personality and ratting skills kept them close to people.

During the mid 1800s, the cat fancy hobby began to emerge, and with it, a popularity for Maine coon cats. Although early cat fancy included showing and displaying cats, the exhibitions had a circuslike atmosphere and judging was much less standardized and structured compared to cat shows today. The Maine coon breed did very well in the nascent period of exhibiting cats and as the enthusiasm for cat fancy of all breeds spread out of the Northeast, so did the Maine coon.

In the early 1900s, other long-haired breeds started to become more popular, especially the Persian. As the enthusiasm among judges and cat lovers for this breed rose exponentially, the enthusiasm for the Maine coon cat declined rapidly. For the first five or six decades of this century, the Maine coon cat was largely ignored, except for a few ardent New England supporters of their native cat.

This red silver classic tabby is a perfect example of the standard set forth by the Maine Coon Breeders and Fanciers' Association.

In the early 1960s, a few of these supporters organized into a loosely structured association and began the work necessary to return the Maine coon cat to popularity. From this group emerged the Maine Coon Breeders and Fanciers' Association (MCBFA), which is today the largest and most influential organization to promote the breed. The MCBFA breed standards are recognized around the world, and their code of rules and ethics are followed by hundreds of breeders who remain devoted to the cat who is as much a part of this nation's heritage as Plymouth Rock. Today the popularity of Maine coon cats is resurging in cat shows across the country and abroad, even among the ardent Persian enthusiasts. Maine coon kit-

The Maine coon's fluffy long hair makes the cat appear very heavy.

tens are in demand, especially in Japan and Europe where they are recognized as being as American as denim jeans and rock and roll.

You may ask, "How did the MCBFA bring the breed back?" One of the earliest things the organizers needed was a standard description of Maine coon cat characteristics. It took awhile before a majority in the MCBFA and the governing parties in all the cat fancy association could agree on the important points. Once a standard was decided, cats could be registered, beginning with Maine coon cats with known pedigree. A pedigree is a family tree that shows a cat's ancestry and the matings that took place to produce offspring leading up to a specific cat. The pedigree verifies that a Maine coon cat is descended entirely from matings between Maine coon cats. *A pedigree designates that a cat is gen-erally recognized to possess characteristics typical of a breed, but it does not verify quality or health in any way!*

Nonpedigreed Maine coon cats were also registered as foundation cats. A foundation cat was one that met the breed standards and three generations of offspring bred with pedigreed Maine coon cats did also. Offspring born after three generations were then considered purebred. Breed registry for foundation stock was open for several years and then closed. All Maine coon cats are now descendants of these cats. The MCBFA rules no longer permit registration of foundation cats nor do they permit outcrossing of Maine coon cats with other breeds.

Who actually registers cats? A Maine coon cat registry is kept by several cat fancier associations in North America. Some of these include: the oldest association, the American Cat Association (ACA); the American Cat Fanciers Association (ACFA); the Cat Club of America (CCA); the Cat Fanciers Federation (CFF); the largest association, Cat Fanciers' Association, Inc. (CFA); and The International Cat Association (TICA), with whom the Maine coon cat is perhaps the most popular. Maine coon cats are also registered with the Canadian Cat Association (CCA), and with the Governing Council of the Cat Fancy (GCCF) in Great Britain and the Federation Internationale Feline (FIFe) in France, which registers Maine coons all over Europe. These groups and others keep track of Maine coon breeding and showing throughout the world. Breeders will register cats with one or more associations depending upon the cat shows in which they wish to exhibit and campaign their cats.

MCBFA Standard

The following detailed description is taken from the MCBFA information booklet about their favorite felines.

General statement: The Maine coon is a solid, rugged cat and is America's oldest natural long-haired breed. Type must not be sacrificed for size, nor size for type, the optimum being a large, typey cat. Females are somewhat smaller than males, and allowance should be made for the slow maturation of the breed.

Head: The head is medium in length and width, with a squareness to the muzzle. Allowance should be made for broadening in males. Cheekbones should be high. The nose is medium in length with a gentle, concave curve and no break or bump. The chin is firm and in line with the upper lip and nose.

Eyes: The eyes should be large, wide set, and slightly oblique in setting. Eye color can be shades of green, gold, or copper, though white cats may be blue or odd-eyed. There

is no relationship between eye color and coat color. Clarity of eye color is desirable.

Ears: Large, wide at the base, moderately pointed, and well-tufted, the ears should be set high on the head approximately an ear's width apart. Lynxlike tipping is desirable.

Body: Muscular, medium to large in size, and broad chested, the body is long, with all parts in proportion, creating a rectangular appearance. When viewed from the rear, there is a definite squareness to the rump. The neck is medium-long.

Legs and paws: The legs should be substantial, wide set, and medium in length, contributing to a rectangular appearance. The paws should be large, round, and well tufted (five toes in front, four toes in back).

Coat: The fur on the shoulders is short, gradually increasing in length along the back and sides, ending in full britches and long, shaggy belly fur. The fur is soft but has body, falls smoothly, and lies close to the body. A slight undercoat is carried. A full ruff is not expected; however, there should be a frontal ruff beginning at the base of the ears.

Coat color: All recognized colors. White trim around the chin and lip is permitted, except in solid color cats.

Disqualifications: Buttons, lockets, spots, overall even coat, short cobby body, crossed eyes, kinked tail, and incorrect number of toes are disqualifications.

Penalties: Delicate bone structures, untufted paws, poor condition, a nose break or bump, an undershot chin, and a short rounded muzzle are penalties.

As detailed as this description may seem, there is still a lot of room for interpretation of the standard by judges and breeders that determines each Maine coon cat's potential in the show ring. What is medium, wide, firm, or tufted to one person may not be so to another.

These differences in interpretation of the breed standard between judges in each of the cat fancier associations has led to at least two and possibly more recognized types of Maine coon cat: the "sweet-looking" variety and the "feral-looking" variety that you may be told about when you are searching for the perfect kitten to take home.

And, at any point in time, judges and breeders may place emphasis on certain of the physical characteristics over others, such as the size and placement of the ears or conformation of the chin. As a novice, some of the subtle differences between one cat and another may be lost to you, however, they will be of great significance to the breeder who must anticipate the show potential of each kitten to determine which ones will enter a breeding program and which ones will be sold as pets. Although it is important for breeders to achieve that special look in their cats with just the right size ears and chins and whatnot, all would agree that the healthy, rugged, practical origins of the Maine coon cat should not be forfeited.

Big but Not Gargantuan

As one breeder put it, "A male Maine coon cat in full coat regalia is something to behold!" There are a lot of people out there that think Maine coon cats weigh-in at 30 or 40 pounds, and that simply isn't so. The average female Maine coon weighs between 8 and 12 pounds (3.6–5.4 kg). A really large female will weigh up to 14 pounds (6.4 kg). Male Maine coon cats weigh upward of 12 to 18 pounds (5.4–8.2 kg). There have been lean males and females that weigh more than those ranges, however, they are the exception and heavier cats are likely to be obese.

Considering that the average domestic shorthair house cat weighs about 8 to 10 pounds (3.6–4.5 kg),

Maine coon cats are still formidably large. And they will indeed look gargantuan at a cat show when compared to a lithe Oriental shorthair. Maine coons do not reach their maximum body size until four or five years of age. Genetics, diet, and exercise all contribute to the cat's overall size. Intact male cats are generally more likely to achieve their fullest genetic potential due to sex hormone contributions to development, however, breeding males often lose coat density and body, which can make them look smaller.

Notice also that unlike breed descriptions of dogs, there are no height or length standards for the Maine coon. If asked about that, breeders will refer to the importance of the cat's overall rectangular body shape or tail proportions instead of the cat's dimensions, although many will tell of Maine coons that have measured 5 feet (1.5 m) from nose to tail.

Although all colors are accepted by the MCBFA, the brown tabby, with either classic or mackerel markings, is still the most common and favored color of Maine coon cats. Colorpoints such as those occurring in the Siamese or Himalayan breeds are not acceptable.

Health Problems Within the Breed

For the most part, the Maine coon cat has been and remains a vigorous and healthy breed with no more susceptibility to disease than any nonpedigreed domestic cat. This is fortunate because although controlled breeding selects for many desirable traits and characteristics, it brings along undesirable ones as well. Although small problems like kinked tails and crossed eyes may be of little problem to the cat, consider, for example, the increased incidence of respiratory diseases in Persians or the susceptibility

Maine coon cats come in a wide variety of colors, but the brown tabby remains the most common and favored.

to the cold in the thin-coated rex. Some breeders feel that at the time the registry was closed, the number of Maine coon foundation cats was sufficiently large to prevent the problems associated with line-breeding and a small gene pool. Others feel that without the introduction of new foundation cats, genetically related faults and lower disease resistance could begin to show up within the breed.

Two such health problems are currently being watched by Maine coon cat enthusiasts: cardiomyopathy and hip dysplasia. Cardiomyopathy is a disease of the heart muscle that results in heart failure and throm-boembolism (clot formation similar to stroke). The disease occurs in several forms in humans, dogs, and cats, and probably other species as well, and it has clearly been demonstrated to be a heritable condition. Cardiomyopathy can go undetected for a long period of time and the condition can exist in a mild, nonfatal form in some animals and thus lies the problem. Some of these clinically normal animals can be used for breeding and may pass along the tendency to develop cardiomyopathy to their offspring.

Not at all surprising is that cardiomyopathy has been seen in Maine coon cats as it has been seen in other breeds too. No one knows just how many Maine coon cats may be affected. Cardiomyopathy is diagnosed using ultrasound technology, which is available to veterinarians. Currently there are no standard guidelines or MCBFA recommendations for screening breeding cats for this disease, although some breeders have begun on their own to test their cats. You do not need to be alarmed about this disease, but you should be aware of its importance within this breed and within the general cat population.

Maine coon cat breeders are also concerned about the incidence of hip dysplasia. Historically, this has solely been of concern to dog breeders but it is well known to veterinarians that cats, too, including Maine coon cats, can have this bony malformation of the hips. This is an enormously complex condition related not only to genetics but also to environmental factors. The significance of hip dysplasia in the cat is not known and it is in the incipient stages of study. Again, there are no guidelines for screening or certification of cats like there are in dogs. You need not be alarmed about hip dysplasia; simply be aware of its occurrence and watch for more information to become available in the future.

Selecting the Perfect Companion

Considerations Before Acquiring

So, you've gone to a cat show or two or maybe you've seen pictures and articles in cat fancy magazines or you've met a friend's Maine coon cat and now you've fallen in love. Living one more day without all that fluff and energy is more than you can bear. Before you run out and get yourself a Maine coon kitten, there are a few things for everyone in your household to consider.

• **Do you really want a pet?** Accepting a pet of any species into your home is a big, long commitment,

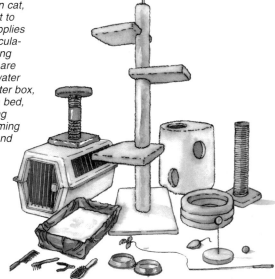

When considering the purchase of a Maine coon cat, don't forget to include supplies in your calculations. Among the basics are food and water bowls, a litter box, a carrier, a bed, a scratching post, grooming supplies, and toys.

nearly twenty years. It will be a life-changing event, not to the magnitude of marriage or the birth of a new sibling of course, but no matter, your life will never be the same. You now must be responsible, which to some people is an ugly word. *Owning a pet is a privilege not a right.*

• **Do you really want a cat?** Cats are not dogs, birds, reptiles, or fish. A cat is a uniquely individual creature, one of great dignity and self-respect. Cats are not really loners as some would say; when they act aloof, they just think they're better than you. They crave attention, but perhaps not always physical contact. Some want you to play with them, some prefer that you just look admiringly in their direction and think "My, what a fine cat!" Unlike your cocker spaniel, your Maine coon cat will not lie at your feet in devotion. Most of what your pet will do will be to amuse itself, and if you enjoy its antics, well that's just fine. Your devotion is nothing more than what your cat deserves.

• **Do you really want a purebred cat?** People who purchase purebred cats (or dogs) often have one big misconception and that is they assume that just because the cat has papers or a pedigree that it is a good animal. Papers, designating that a cat is purebred, in no way, shape, or form guarantee quality. By quality, I mean how healthy that cat is or how representative it is of the breed, and how the cat would stand up to the scrutiny of a judge's evaluation. A pedigree says absolutely nothing about the current or future health of the cat or its suitability for breeding. A pedigree simply reflects the cat's genetic makeup. The best reason for wanting a purebred cat is because you love the looks and personality of your chosen favorite—in this case, the Maine coon.

The worst reason for wanting a purebred cat is for profit. Breeding cats or any other animal is at best a break-even proposition and should be pursued only after considerable study and preparation.

• **Do you have the time for a Maine coon cat?** No, you won't have to slog on galoshes to walk your cat in the winter, but caring for your Maine coon will require some time. Time is needed to provide food and water once or twice a day and to tend to the litter box. Your Maine coon will require a certain amount of grooming, including combing and an occasional nail trim. And then there's the matter of exercise and play; a kitten needs no encouragement to turn somersaults and catapult from the cat tree, but your adult Maine coon cat might need some coaxing. You can't ignore your pet if it drops a ball in your lap and wants to play fetch even if you are dead tired after work. And think of the exercise you'll get fishing all those tinfoil balls out from under the couch.

• **Are you aware of the cost?** The initial cost for your Maine coon kitten will be substantial. If you purchase your kitten from out-of-state, you will also be responsible for all transportation costs involved in getting your kitten home. You will also need to purchase a litter box, and possibly bowls, a bed, grooming supplies, a carrier, and toys. Ongoing expenses include food and veterinary care. Veterinary medical care will be greater during the first year because your kitten may need several vaccinations and will be neutered.

Before selecting a Maine coon kitten, visit several catteries and interview the breeders. Reputable breeders also interview potential purchasers.

• **Your Maine coon cat will need care when you travel.** If you travel away from home for longer than a day or two someone will need to come into your home and care for your pet or your cat will need to go into a kennel. Unless you have helpful neighbors, these services cost money and must be arranged well ahead of time during busy times like holidays.

• **Are you prepared to keep your Maine coon cat indoors?** Most good breeders are going to ask you to agree to this as a condition of sale.

• **Do you want a pet- or show-quality Maine coon kitten?** Which is better, pet- or show-quality? Well that depends upon your preference and your pocketbook. Show-quality Maine coon kittens cost significantly more than pet-quality. No matter, maybe you've always wanted to drive a certain car, or achieve the highest academic level in your class, but could never realize those dreams. Well here's a chance to have the best. If you think you'd like to show your Maine coon cat, then acquiring a show-quality kitten is desirable.

Maine coon cats not only come in a variety of colors but also with many different kinds of markings. These two sport black and white patches.

If it is important to you that your Maine Coon be a stellar example of the breed, then you should do your homework and talk to several breeders. Remember that pet or show designations are largely based on physical appearance and subtle differences that you may not be able to appreciate anyway! Quality designations are given when kittens are young and are at best an educated guess based on the breeder's experience. Sometimes a cat that wasn't expected to be so gorgeous actually grows up to be spectacular. As one breeder said, not intending to be boastful, "I really sell only show-quality anyway." It's just that all her cats were so beautiful, each one of them was a joy. So as you look at a litter in choosing a kitten, inspecting every swirl and every tuft, remember that it's a kitten's personality that may ultimately engage your attention.

Where to Acquire

A cattery is more than just a facility that breeds cats. A cattery is a breeder with a serious devotion toward breeding, raising, and showing a specific breed of cat. A cattery is not defined by the number of animals owned or bred at the facility, but rather by the level of involvement the breeder has in promoting the breed overall. Within the world of Maine coon cats, the cattery breeder is likely, but not always, to be a member in some capacity of the Maine Coon Breeders and Fanciers' Association (MCBFA) (see Associations, page 108). And although a Maine coon cattery breeder doesn't have to be a member of this organization to be recognized by colleagues as a good breeder, they will none-the-less support and abide by the rules and ethics established by this group.

A reputable cattery breeder is the best source for acquiring a Maine coon cat. These are serious individuals who carefully select cats for their breeding programs in order to strengthen the chances of producing the most desirable Maine coon cat traits and characteristics in each breeding while diminishing recognized faults as well. The cats chosen for breeding are chosen both on the basis of appearance and conformation as well as temperament and personality, so cattery breeders spend much of their time studying their own cats as well as other breeders' cats. Cattery breeders participate in national and international cat fancier association-sponsored cat shows and follow a network of information in newsletters and other cat-related periodicals that relates to current trends in the breed. They know what judges are looking for in competition and who the winning cats are, and they try to introduce similar cats into their own lines.

Aside from their preoccupation with breeding and showing Maine coon kittens and cats of the highest quality, cattery breeders are very concerned about the health of the kittens. A kitten or cat acquired from a cattery should have been examined by a veterinarian. It should have begun the series of inoculations against several infectious diseases at the time of purchase and be guaranteed free from carrying feline leukemia virus. All reputable breeders

This Maine coon is tricolored, with brown and cinnamon patches and a solid white chin and chest.

give a health guarantee. A reputable cattery breeder will recognize the importance of early handling and socialization and sell only kittens and cats whose temperament make them suitable as pets.

Warning: Not every Maine coon cattery will put the health and well-being of the breed first in their motives for selling kittens. Although most cattery breeders are spiritually devoted to the cats, a few individuals engage in breeding for lesser motives. You should be cautious about purchasing a kitten from any breeder interested in a quick sell, one who is reticent about revealing husbandry and breeding practices.

Finding a good cattery breeder: Catteries register their names with one or more of the several national and international cat fancier associations (see Associations, page 108.) Although these clubs do not make endorsements, they can refer you to the catteries; it will be up to you to screen the breeders. In addition, these associations sponsor cat shows through local clubs. By attending a cat show, you will have the opportunity to talk to a number of breeders in person and see some of their cats. This is an excellent way of getting information about Maine coon cats. You don't have to be a breeder or even a Maine coon cat owner to subscribe to the MCBFA's periodical, *The Scratch Sheet* which lists breeders and their addresses; you simply have to love Maine coon cats!

A number of magazines devoted to all breeds of cats are published monthly or bimonthly. Aside from the valuable information contained in the articles, you will find breeders who advertise their kittens in these periodicals. Occasionally a good breeder will advertise in the newspaper; however, this form of advertisement is more commonly used by a casual breeder and you should be cautious of kittens acquired through this source.

Don't overlook friends and acquaintances who already own Maine coon cats as a source of information about breeders. They can give you firsthand background about their own experi-

Children should be taught the proper way to handle a kitten.

ences in finding that perfect kitten. Your veterinarian may also be familiar with a good cattery.

Do your homework: Once you have a few breeders' names, make a list of questions about the cattery that you think are important to ask. Include the following in your list:
• MCBFA member and/or supporter?
• How long has the cattery been in existence?
• What color/gender of kittens are available?
• How often does the cattery have kittens?
• Age of kittens at purchase?
• Terms of purchase?
• Is a health guarantee offered?
• What prepurchase veterinary care is given?
• Incidence of infectious diseases in the cattery, including feline leukemia virus and feline infectious peritonitis virus?
• If out-of-state, how is the kitten transported?
• Cost of purchase?
• Can you visit the cattery?

During your conversation with each breeder, try to get a sense of purpose for why this person breeds Maine coon cats. If the reason for breeding hedges toward profit, beware! Breeding is a labor intensive and expensive undertaking and monetary rewards are few. A substantial profit is received only when a compromise is made in the health and well-being of the animals. These animals are often overbred with little attention given to improving the breed overall.

Ask each breeder to describe his or her husbandry practices and philosophy. Note any breeders who appear fanatically dogmatic about their beliefs. After a while, you will recognize those who may appear extreme in their thinking and practices. Although everyone has ways of approaching breeding that are based on their own circumstances, experience, and research, certain basic practices will be consistent from one breeder to the next. As an example, everyone would agree that nutrition is important and breeders will have their individual favorite diets to recommend. Raise a wary eye to the one who eschews the work of commercial pet food research and insists that you feed your cat only a home-cooked or vegetarian diet! Eccentricities such as this regarding breeding and care can be harmful.

Determine the breeder's attitude toward and relationship with his or her veterinarian. It should not be adversarial. A reputable breeder will work closely with a veterinary medical doctor to insure the health of the kittens and minimize infectious diseases within the cattery. Breeders who try to "go it alone" and do their own veterinary care often neglect important preventative health matters.

The MCBFA breed standard for Maine coon cats is interpreted slightly differently between the breeders and judges in each cat fancier association (see MCBFA Standard, page 10.) For example, one breeder may have cats with the "sweeter look" favored by CFA judges. A TICA breeder will show cats that fit the "feral" appearance that they prefer. Both types fall within the MCBFA breed standard for Maine coon cats, although one judge may favor one look over another in a show. You should decide what you like best and inquire about what look is offered at each cattery if you indeed have a preference.

Another major consideration, of course, is availability of kittens of a specific gender or bearing a coat color and pattern for which you have a particular preference. This is a secondary consideration for many people, because every Maine coon kitten has

The correct way to hold a kitten is to support its hindquarters with one hand and to hold its chest steady with the other hand.

the potential to grow up to be the lovely and intelligent cat that is so popular, regardless of the sex or coat color. Still, if you have your heart set on having a red classic tabby female, your breeder search will have to begin with those whose cats have the genetics to produce red tabby offspring. Again, cat shows are an excellent place to admire Maine coon cats of all colors. You may just change your mind!

The only way you will know if a breeder is a good one or not will be to interview as many breeders as you can. Select the breeder who seems to be knowledgeable in many areas of Maine coon cat breeding and showing. Your breeder should be eager to talk about the cats and the cattery. He or she should have certain specific standards for the homes in which their kittens are placed; they should not be extreme. The breeder should follow the ethics and standards of the MCBFA. Keep in mind that your relationship with

Maine coon cats can also be solid-colored, or almost solid. This black smoke cat is a dramatic example.

the breeder may not end with the sale and purchase of a kitten.

Unless a breeder is well known within the Maine coon cat community with a well-recognized reputation for caring and quality, you should visit the cattery to see the facilities and the kittens. The cattery should be clean and free from odors. Adult cats should be kept separate from young kittens. Recently queened cats and their kittens should also be isolated from other cats. Segregation of the cats is important in prevention of infectious diseases, especially in young animals.

Observe the cats and kittens for evidence of illness. You shouldn't hear any sneezing and there shouldn't be any runny noses or eyes. A good cattery will vaccinate its breeding cats regularly for infectious diseases and take the necessary precautions to prevent the introduction of viruses including feline leukemia virus (FeLV) and feline immunodeficiency virus (FIV). A

good cattery will not sell kittens knowingly infected with ear mites, intestinal parasites, or ringworm.

As in any breed of dog or cat, there are a few catteries that really stand out in reputation among their peers and colleagues. The names of these breeders will become known to you in your search for just that perfect kitten. If a cattery is well respected and especially if it is located some distance from you, it is usually safe to choose a kitten based on photographs.

The breeder will interview you: Reputable breeders interview and select the owners to whom they sell kittens as carefully as they plan the breedings, trying to match the right kitten into the right home. Because breeders care deeply about the kittens they sell, they will assess the homes where the kittens are placed. This is a required practice by the MCBFA.

Good breeders want kittens to go to loving homes where they will receive the attention and care that they deserve. They may ask you about other cats and pets you have at home. Breeders want to make sure that kittens are not placed into harmful or neglectful circumstances and many will request that you agree to keeping your Maine coon cat exclusively indoors. Unless a kitten is being sold to someone who is seriously committed to campaigning and showing, they will also insist that the kitten is not to be bred. Most breeders require that a kitten be spayed or neutered at the earliest appropriate age and will withhold registration papers and the pedigree until proof of surgery is provided by a veterinarian. Some breeders will require that they retain showing and breeding rights to kittens who display particular promise at the time of sale.

Some will also require that the purchaser return any cat to the cattery, regardless of age, if the purchaser can no longer keep the cat. Situations where this might happen include having to move, if someone develops an allergy, or if the new kitten isn't accepted by existing cats in the household.

Acquiring an adult cat: Catteries are the best source for an adult Maine coon cat if a kitten is not an appropriate or desirable choice for a household. Breeders look to place their adults cats into good homes after they are "retired" from breeding. These cats must be spayed or neutered, and may be given to a good home or sold at a substantially lower price than a kitten.

The casual breeder: Another source of kittens might be the casual, sometimes called "backyard," breeders, those who own a Maine coon cat and decide to breed it to another for any number of reasons. They may want an offspring of their own cat for sentimental reasons, or they may have friends who have fallen in love with the breed and wish to have one of their own. A desire to have the children "witness the miracle of birth" is also often given by casual breeders as a reason for mating their pet.

This youngster has odd-colored eyes, a quirk not uncommon in solid white Maine coons.

At a cat show, every inch of a Maine coon is examined to determine how close to the standard it comes. The casual owner does not need a perfect cat.

Regarding casual breeders as a source for a Maine coon kitten, beware! Casual breeding of any pet, regardless of the species or breed contributes substantially to the unwanted pet population worldwide. You may find it hard to understand how you would be adding to this problem by purchasing a kitten from a casual Maine coon cat fancier. ("I'm buying one, aren't I? Not abandoning one!") In fact, by purchasing a kitten from a casual breeder, you are encouraging the breeding of cats by individuals who are not educated about the responsibilities of these matters. Casual breedings seldom improve the breed through careful selection of parent conformation and temperament. Kittens are often placed in homes eager to have them at first, only to be discarded later when families move, students return home at the semester's end, or when one member of the household grows tired of having to "take care of the cat."

It is doubtful that a serious Maine coon cat breeder would sell a kitten, pet- or show-quality, without a spay or neuter agreement to anyone except another breeder. Casual breeders in possession of an intact male or female Maine coon cat are apt to have such a cat either because they broke an agreement with a serious breeder, or obtained the cat from a less-than-reputable source. As such, it is improbable that casual breeders would be breeding a Maine coon cat of genuine quality. In fact, they may not possess registration papers verifying the pedigree. Therefore, if you wish to purchase a kitten from such a casual breeder, you may not be purchasing a pedigree Maine coon kitten and you are certainly unlikely to be acquiring one that is truly representative of the breed.

You should also scrutinize the premises of the casual breeder for cleanliness, attention to basic veterinary care, and health problems in the parents prior to purchase, just as you should a serious cattery breeder. Without the support of an informed, knowledgeable breeder, prepurchase

The Maine coon's pretty eyes are a distinguishing feature of the breed. When selecting a kitten for adoption, make sure the eyes, as well as the nose, are free of discharge. The ears should also be clean, and the youngster should not sneeze.

preventative health care, health guarantee, and other ethical considerations, a kitten from a casual breeder seems like a poor choice. You might as well get a mutt-cat.

Pet stores: The MCBFA does not endorse the sale of Maine coon kittens and cats through pet retail facilities. The MCBFA code of ethics requires that breeders interview prospective owners to make sure that the kittens are going into loving and suitable homes, which is of course not possible if the kittens are sold through a pet store. Therefore, a Maine coon kitten sold through a pet store has probably not been bred at a facility that supports the ethics and principles of the MCBFA. This leaves open questions about the health of the breeding stock, sanitation, and preventative health care as well. You should be cautious about acquiring a Maine coon kitten through a pet retail facility.

Consider adopting two kittens. They would keep each other company.

Animal shelters: Believe it or not, a significant percentage of the animal population in animal shelters consists of purebred animals. You can call around to various shelters and humane organizations and ask to be notified if a Maine coon cat comes in. Or you can make a visit to the facility and take a look for yourself. Even if the cat didn't come with papers, it may exhibit some of the charming characteristics of the breed, and that may be good enough! You may be giving a reprieve to an adult cat that would otherwise be euthanized.

Cost

Cost is a highly variable figure and depends on the source, age, and quality of the Maine coon that you choose. There is some regional variation in price between areas of the United States, and prices are higher for kittens that are sold internationally. The price for the occasional Maine coon kitten that may be sold at a pet store will be high regardless of the quality. Cattery prices will vary depending upon the reputation of the breeder and the cats, of course. Offspring of Supreme Grand Champion cats will cost more to buy. However, adult cats that have been retired from breeding are usually placed into homes at bargain prices and are often given away to suitable pet homes. Most shelters have a small adoption fee and/or fee for neutering.

The current cost range for a pet-quality Maine coon kitten is $400 to $550. Cost for show-quality kittens begins around $800. You will also pay all expenses associated with transportation if a kitten is shipped. The price of Maine coon kittens sold to Japan and Europe begin at $1,500 to $2,000 plus transportation fees and tariffs.

Age for Acquiring

I've often said and many agree that kittens are better than television. They

Many houses are home to both a Maine coon cat and a dog.

can entertain you with their curiosity of all things visible and much that is not. They can make you laugh when they hop sideways and bushy-tailed after the dog. The best age to acquire a new Maine coon kitten is no younger than eight weeks of age. Earlier acquisition deprives a kitten of the valuable play experience with its littermates that is needed for proper socialization. In my experience, kittens acquired before eight weeks of age may play overly aggressively with humans, probably because they were never taught the rules of play by littermates, and may also be more shy around strangers or inappropriately aggressive when they perceive themselves to be threatened.

It follows that for a kitten to be accepting of human contact, it should be exposed to handling early in its life, and especially between the ages of two to 12 weeks. In animal shelters, pet stores, or catteries with large numbers of animals, the kittens may not receive adequate handling to properly socialize them to humans. Feral barn cats and their kittens are an example

Choosing the Kitten

The kitten you choose should, before all else, be healthy. Healthy kittens are bright, alert, and responsive to their environment. They should be willing and eager to engage in play with you and their littermates. Their movements and play should be well coordinated, and their curiosity keen.

The eyes and nose of the kitten you choose should be free from discharge, and there is no sneezing allowed! The ears should be clean and without wax or black debris that suggests a mite infestation. The average eight-week-old kitten weighs about 1.5 to 2 pounds (0.7–0.9 kg). A smaller kitten does not necessarily mean an unhealthy one, but it may be younger than suggested. A good breeder will have accurate birth dates.

The choice of a male or female kitten is a personal one; kittens of both gender grow up to be excellent cat companions. Males and females are equally affectionate and responsible about the litter box. Personally, I find that males are more easygoing, even sometimes goofy, and take particularly well to other animals and cats. Females are often more dignified and assertive with their rights as more intelligent beings, and can be more territorial around the house.

One or More?

Maine coon cats are noted for their acceptance of other pets, including other cats. Breeders will be the first to tell you of the harmoniously coexistent lives their cats lead. Certainly this is true or there wouldn't be any catteries. But Maine coons are still cats, nonetheless, and as a rule, cats hold limited regard for the social graces. The only felines to live in group societies are lions that live together in prides. Most other cats prefer to be the sole ruler of their territory or house, and owner of the people therein.

A coloring favored by many Maine coon enthusiasts is red mackerel.

of this. One must catch the kittens early in order to tame them to be successful pets. For this reason, if you choose a kitten older than 12 or 14 weeks, be sure to inquire about how much handling the kitten has received. It should give you insight into the potential personality as an adult.

Charming as they may be, kittens are not for everyone. An older or adult cat who is perfectly content with dozing on a lap, may be a better companion for an elderly person than a leg-climbing, nickknack-toppling youngster.

When trying to pick that perfect companion, color should not be an obstacle, as these four kittens show.

Cats do not have any familial memories. In the natural scheme of things, kittens from a litter will eventually disperse to live alone, except to mate. Unlike puppies who remember their littermates and will recognize each other when reunited after separation, cats do not. So if you bring a new kitten or cat into the house with an established cat, whether or not they get along will depend entirely on the cats. They may become friends and companions in mischief, and groom each other and sleep in a pile, or they may torment one another despite any effort on your part to reason with them.

And, it's very hard to tell ahead of time what the outcome of bringing another kitten or cat into the household will be. You may not be aware of how possessive the established cat is until faced with the prospect of sharing. Sharing is not a common word in

the cat vocabulary and your first cat's response will depend upon the age and/or gender of the new cat that you are introducing. A pair of neutered male Maine coons, or a mixed pair with one male and one female may get along better than two females. In a mixed pair, you may find that the male takes great delight in teasing his "sister."

Kittens and young cats are more playful and interactive than older adults. A youngster will naturally try to engage the adults in play, which may or not be well received. An older cat may ignore the solicitations of the younger one, or even become aggressive toward it. If you decide to get another kitten or cat, do so because you want it, not because you think your cat is lonesome while you're at work and would appreciate the company of another of its species—trust me, your pet won't. Also keep in mind that you should have two of everything, especially two litter boxes if your cats will not have access to the outdoors.

Two kittens: This is the most successful pairing of one or more cats in a household, although I will warn you: No matter how many people live in your house, two kittens will have you outnumbered. Although it's not necessary to chose littermates, try to choose kittens close in age. Matched-age kittens are more likely to be at the same stage of development both physically and socially. Both kittens should be playing similar games and interacting with equal interest and intensity. An older kitten who is beginning to become independent and more solitary in its activities may rebuff a younger one who is still very much interested in "hunting" and playing with other kittens.

Kittens mismatched in age can still become friends but it may take longer. Matching age is much more important than matching gender, especially if the kittens are eventually to be neutered. If these kittens are confined to a limited territory, especially if that territory is a house, they will be more inclined to work out a sharing arrangement and remain close companions. If allowed outdoors, they will probably stay friendly but may not be as chummy because of the natural instinct to disperse.

Introducing a New Kitten or Cat

There's a variety of techniques for making an introduction of your new kitten. One technique is to just bring in the new one, put both cats in the same room and that is that. Behaviorists call that sort of thing "flooding," when an animal is desensitized by overwhelming it with whatever the stimulus is that the animal is anxious about. In this case, the established cat is "flooded" by the presence

of the new cat or kitten. The established one will likely hiss and make a fuss and look at you pleadingly to get rid of the creature. There may be a chase and tumble and a little lost fur. This is not a good technique if blood is drawn. Eventually, if they're going to get along with one another, both pets will do so by establishing territories.

Another introduction technique is olfactory without being visual. It also dissociates the presence of the new pet with the owner and that may lessen the resentment of the established cat. Resentment may sound a bit anthropomorphic, but I do think that some cats can be resentful.

Put the new kitten or cat in a room of its own and allow your new pet and the established cat to sniff at one another from under the door for a few days. In the meantime, lavish the established cat with lots of attention. After a few days of being aware of but not actually seeing each other, allow the two to have limited time together. This may be for only a few minutes at first, then gradually lengthen the time over a period of a few days. Be prepared for a least a little bit of fussing on the part of the established cat even with this technique, especially if you are introducing a new kitten.

Maine Coon Cats and Dogs

I have suggested that it could be difficult to introduce another cat into your Maine coon cat's household but, as a breed, Maine coon cats are particularly tolerant of other animals, dogs included. This is especially true of kittens. Lovable dogs such as Labradors and other retrievers will be curious at first and perform the necessary sniffing and tasting to satisfy that curiosity and quickly accept the cat or kitten as a playmate. But within every breed of dog, no matter how lovable, there are some individuals who see cats as prey. An adult cat can probably set the dog straight with a few rapid fire blows to the face, but a kitten could be seriously injured in seconds by an aggressive dog. If that volley of blows targets the eyes, your dog could be injured and even lose its vision. So, no matter what breed of dog you have, always have your dog on a leash and under control when it is first introduced to your new Maine coon cat or kitten. After the introductory period, you will be better able to judge if they are friends or foes.

Maine Coon Cats and Other Pets

Just as kittens who grow up with other kittens or cats learn tolerance of them, so do kittens who are raised with other species of animals. Kittens who live with birds, rabbits, guinea pigs, or other pocket pets are likely to remain at least aloof if not friendly to these animals as the kitten grows to an adult. Most cats have good sense when it comes to psittacines (parakeets, parrots, and macaws), and stay clear of them, especially the larger ones.

The smile on this young lady's face shows that she feels she has found the "perfect companion."

This Maine coon youngster has staked its claim— high up on an antique desk in front of a large window letting in warm rays of sunshine.

Supplies

Food and Water Bowls

Your cat should have separate bowls for food and water that should be easy to keep clean. Water bowls should be reasonably spill-proof; some are weighted on the bottom for stability. Pet dishes are made from plastic, stainless steel, porcelain, or glass. The material is irrelevant unless your cat is sensitive to the dyes in the plastics, although this is not a common problem in cats. Cats prone to feline acne should be fed on a flat surface like a saucer or paper plate to avoid rubbing the chin into the food or on the sloped sides of the bowl as the cat eats. But whether you use an empty margarine tub or a hand-thrown, personalized crock is not as important as the food you choose to put inside it.

Food and water should be served in separate bowls that are easy to clean. Weighted water bowls are available to reduce spills.

Litter Boxes and Fillers

Cat owners have more choices than ever in this category of supplies. And because house soiling is the number one behavior problem that cat owners bring to the attention of their veterinarian, this is one of the most important choices that you will make. Actually, your Maine coon cat should make the choice.

A litter box can be as simple as a cardboard box with the sides cut down and can be discarded after use. There are also commercially available disposable boxes. These are particularly nice for travel. A more conventional setup is a plastic open or covered tray. Covered trays ensure privacy and have a replaceable filter in the lid to help control odors. Despite the privacy factor, cats generally prefer the open box, possibly because the odor becomes trapped and intense under the cover. You can purchase any of these items at pet retail outlets, discount stores, and supermarkets.

Traditional clay-type cat litters are economical and still the most common filler used to collect waste. Newer to the marketplace, "clumping" fillers are often based on the naturally clumping bentonite and montmorillonite types of clay that are manufactured to a sand-like consistency. When the cat urinates into the litter, the wet particles adhere to one another and are removed in a solid mass with a slotted scoop, along with the feces. As the litter is used up, the box is replenished with fresh filler. This can be a big advantage for apartment-dwelling cat owners as it is easier to dispose of smaller volumes of litter at a time. Some clumping litters are flushable, but you should follow the directions on the label for proper disposal. Clumping litters keep the litter box cleaner than traditional clay litter because both urine and feces can be removed daily.

Clumping litters are supposed to make taking care of the box easier because, in theory, it never needs to be completely changed—just replenished. I find that this is not really the case, because soft clumping or high traffic through the box causes the clumps to fall apart, leaving soiled litter behind. Eventually, bacteria start to break down the urine, releasing ammonia and other volatile odors and the filler needs to be completely changed. How often this is needed depends on the deodorizing system in the brand of litter and how frequently you scoop.

The biggest drawback to clumping litters is the fine consistency and the tendency for the particles to become caught between the cat's toes and get tracked all over the house. This is particularly a problem with the Maine coon cat's tufted paws. A piece of indoor-outdoor carpet or artificial turf placed outside of the box will help to trap the particles. There are also commercially made trays that fit in front of the litter box, with ridges on their surface that spread the cat's toes and release the litter. Any of those devices will help contain the tracking problem, provided your cat will walk over the textured surface. More than one person has described to me how their cats sail gleefully out of the box and over anything that is placed in front of it.

There are several non-clay litters available; most are pellets made from recycled newspapers. These litters are appealing to cat owners because they are completely biodegradable (some are flushable) and therefore environmentally friendly, but many cats don't like pelleted litter because they can't dig in it very

Litter boxes come in all shapes and colors. The most common is a plastic tray, either open or covered. Covered trays provide privacy and control odors.

well. The "dig-ability" is a big reason why cats like the clumping litters so much.

Some cats prefer shredded newspaper or a flat surface to any form of pellets, clay, or paper. There is also at least one litter box system using recyclable materials as well. The Dry System manufactured by The Sweet "P" Corporation uses a gravel filter over absorbent pads. The pads are discarded and the gravel is washed. This system is relatively new and has a few drawbacks related to handling the solid waste and cleaning the gravel. If you are interested in a product like this, you can contact the company by calling 1-800-937-9909, ask your local pet retailer, check the advertising section of cat magazines, or look for a vendor at a cat show.

Manufacturers incorporate deodorizing chemicals and cedar into litters to help neutralize, or more-to-the-point, mask smells. Most deodorizers are simply perfumes, and these can be just as irritating to the cat's respiratory tract as the ammonia by-product of bacteria on the urine. Some cats don't like the smell of the deodorizers and will avoid the box. For those reasons, I prefer unscented litters. Germicidal deodorizing systems work somewhat better, but there is no substitute for proper box hygiene.

Litter box management will require that you also purchase something to scoop the waste out of the box. If you plan to use the clumping type of cat litter, purchase the widest and largest scoop that you can find. Wide scoops make it easier to remove the clumps of urine without breaking apart and mixing back into the litter. The scoop should have slots wide enough for the litter particles to fall through, yet retain the waste for disposal. Some brands of scoopable litter specify using a scoop

Kitty teasers are a favorite toy of many Maine coon cats.

A kitty teaser with strips of different colors and a puff of yellow has this Maine coon kitten wary.

made of plastic over metal and vice versa. Check the manufacturer's recommendation for your specific brand.

My tip: Plastic litter box liners are nice to use with all nonclumping litters. They make emptying and cleaning the box much tidier. You can purchase liners in a variety of sizes specifically made for this purpose. I find that cats that dig aggressively in the litter box tend to displace the liner unless the box has a rim or cover that locks the liner into place. An alternative to a liner is a tall kitchen garbage bag, which eliminates the displacement problem and is probably less expensive. Before filling the litter box, place the empty box inside the bag and pat out the air. Now fill the box with the desired amount of litter and use a twistie-tie to close up the bag. When it's time to empty the box, simply untie the twistie and invert the bag.

Housekeeping for your Maine coon cat is simple. Except when using the clumping type litter, the box should be completely emptied and washed at least once a week. Some cats will not use a litter box a second time once it is used at all, and they may want you to wash it daily too! The odor will be the most important factor that determines how frequently the box needs cleaning. Urine is broken down to ammonia gas and your Maine coon cat will be acutely aware of that odor because its little nose will be closer to it than yours.

Use hot, soapy water and a brush, and scrub well. You must rinse the box free of soap or disinfectants thoroughly, as some iodinated disinfectants (e.g., Lysol) are toxic to cats. Avoid strong smelling detergents with fragrances that can absorb into the plastic and linger. Odors that are offensive to your cat may trigger aversion to the box and lead to house soiling.

Kitty teasers with fleece balls come in a variety of bright colors.

Fill the box with approximately 2 inches (5 cm) of the filler of your choice. It is necessary to put only a small amount of litter in the box if it is changed daily. If you are not sure which litter box filler to use at first, you can set up a couple of boxes with a variety of fillers and see which box your cat prefers, or choose the same brand your breeder used at the cattery. Once you (or your cat) make a choice, try to stay with one type and one brand to avoid any problems that your cat may have with changes in routine. Abrupt changes in texture or odor of the filler, size, shape, or placement of the litter box may be objectionable to your Maine coon cat. You should have one litter box for each feline member of your family.

Placement of the litter box is important. Your Maine coon cat will prefer some privacy, but make sure that the box is easily accessible. Don't expect your ten-week-old Maine coon kitten to be able to locate the box in a dark basement at the bottom of a long set of stairs. Older cats may be arthritic and

Another essential is a scooper for the litter box. Use the scooper to remove waste matter from the litter.

forgetful. So make it as easy as possible for your Maine coon to find the box, especially when you first bring your pet home. Try a corner of the bathroom, hall, laundry room, or closet. Be aware of any potential factors that could make your kitten avoid the box in its location, such as the back hall where your exuberant golden retriever comes bounding through the door.

After your cat is a well-established member of the family, then you can gradually move the box to a more acceptable location such as a basement. Even if your Maine coon answers the call of nature by eliminating outdoors, you should have a litter box backup for inclement weather or if your pet is not feeling well. The maddening scenario is when your otherwise "outdoor" cat prefers to come in and use a litter box!

Grooming Needs

Although Maine coon cats possess a long, luxurious coat, unlike some other long-haired breeds, this coat does not require a lot of attention, but you will need to purchase several implements to use for general groom-

ing. A metal comb with long teeth set fairly far apart is indispensable for regular combing. To remove the occasional mat that may form in the coat of some Maine coons with a denser undercoat, a second comb, called a mat comb, with moderately spaced stout teeth is needed to pull the mat from the coat without excessive tension on the healthy hair still in the follicles. (See Grooming, page 46.)

If you have a dog or other cats that go in- and out-of-doors, or if you allow your Maine coon cat access to the outdoors, you should also purchase a flea comb. These combs have thin teeth narrowly set together in order to trap scurrying fleas as the comb is pulled through the coat. Manual removal of fleas along with judicious use of insecticides is part of an effective flea control program.(See HOW-TO: Controlling Fleas, page 50.)

There may be a few instances when your Maine coon cat will need a bath. On the rare occasion that your pet actually gets so dirty that cleaning itself may be more of a project than you'd like to see it undertake (i.e., after stalking mice in your dusty attic), use a mild, general grooming shampoo specifically made for cats. Do not use human shampoos or conditioners that are often too harsh for cats. For a variety of dermatitis or skin conditions, it is best to consult your veterinarian for a specific product.

Regular nail trimming will be part of your Maine coon cat's grooming routine. Several styles of nail trimmers are available at pet retail centers. A folding nail or toenail trimmer found at drugstores is a suitable alternative. (See Nail Trimming, page 49.)

Toys and Other Amusements

Environmental enrichment is very important, especially for cats that stay indoors. Environmental enrichment to your Maine coon might be something as simple as a grocery sack. Some places to look for interesting and unusual toys and the latest in kitty amusements are at the vendor exhibits at cat shows, in the advertising sections of cat magazines, and at pet superstores. Your breeder will have some suggestions for toys, too.

Maine coon cats enjoy the opportunity to exercise with animated toys. Shiny strips of tinsel, feathers, or balsa wood suspended by a piano wire or on rod and reel are called kitty teasers, and Maine coon cats love them. The kitty teaser is interactive and you play, too. Fur- and fleece-covered toys and foam or tinfoil balls that bat nicely make for a good chase across the floor. Kittens in particular like "track toys"—balls that spin out of reach in circular tracks when batted through narrow openings in the casing. Toys that bounce or toys that make noise like a dying mouse catch their attention. String or yarn is not an appropriate toy for cats. Linear objects can cause obstruction and laceration of the esophagus and intestines if swallowed.

Maine coon cats like to be high up on things—your dresser, the top of the refrigerator, the Christmas tree, the fireplace mantle—and so your cat will enjoy a bird feeder in the backyard with a conveniently placed window hammock for observation. And your pet will probably appreciate the squirrels at the feeder more than you will. Carpet-covered climbing trees of various sizes are wonderful exercise if you have the room. Smaller carpeted or fleece tunnels make good hiding places for games of chase. Cat trees and tunnels are especially amusing for people who have more than one Maine coon cat because they can be the backdrop for hilarious gymnastics and efforts to outdo one another.

In my house, we have what has been dubbed the "stack o'cats" by our

Kittens especially like track toys—circular tracks with balls that can be batted through narrow openings. Grocery sacks are also popular.

friend Rob, although the original idea was suggested to me by another veterinarian who uses something similar in the cat boarding room of his hospital. We purchased a 4-foot (1.2 m) ladder and painted it bright red and placed yellow boards across the rungs to make shelves. Each shelf, including the fold-down one for your paint can, is covered with a fluffy rug and each fluffy rug is in turn covered by a cat. Thus the name "stack o'cats!" Naturally, each cat has a preferred perch, the topmost shelf being the most prized because that's at human eye level and affords the best view of the bird feeder.

Scratching posts: It's important that you provide your Maine coon cat with a scratching post. A cat scratches at objects for two reasons: to mark its territory with chemical substances from the sweat glands on the bottom of its feet and to remove old nail sheaths from its

Kitty toys don's have to cost a fortune. A wad of paper is keeping this eight-month-old busy.

Carpet-covered climbing trees and tunnels are the setting for hours of antics and exercise.

A silver patch tabby kitten snuggles into a cozy basket.

Scratching posts come in an assortment of surface materials and designs. Before buying one, observe your kitten for a while to determine what it would probably prefer.

claws. Even declawed cats continue to perform scratching behavior. Cats definitely have a preference for the material and the geometry of the surface that they use for this, so scratching posts are made covered with carpet or jute and can be upright, slanted, or horizontal.

It's almost better to wait to purchase a scratching post until you've had a chance to observe your kitten for a few days to see if your pet will show you its preference. If no preference becomes obvious, then you can make the choice yourself. (See Scratching the Furniture, page 62.) Keep in mind that you may need to buy a different post if you choose incorrectly. Your Maine coon breeder may also have an insight into the right scratching post for your kitten.

Beds

If you want to keep your Maine coon from sleeping on certain pieces of furniture, you'll need to provide your cat with an alternative. Next to being up high, cats like being inside things, especially tight spaces. Plush cat nests and bungalows or baskets with high sides are attractive and cozy sleeping places because a cat can curl up. Sprinkle the inside with a little catnip to attract your pet's interest. Sometimes a cat finds the proffered bed suitable, but just doesn't like its location, so experiment with a few different places. Observe where the sunbeams travel through your home during the day and put your Maine coon's bed along their path.

A Room with a View

One emphasis in this book and from your breeder is to encourage you to keep your Maine coon cat indoors. Some readers may find this offensive and unnatural for the cat, but before you dismiss it entirely, consider that thousands of city and apartment dwelling cats are confined indoors for their whole lives and are utterly content for it.

There is a compromise; that is, bring a little of the outdoors inside. Your cat can have "free access" to the outdoors from the safety of your home if you screen in a porch or deck. You won't need to winterize this space; a cat door can be installed in the existing door or slider. Look for one at pet retail outlets and in catalogs. Also check out the indoor/outdoor playpens created by Freedom Pet Concepts, Inc., 1-800-979-9075.

At greater expense, you could design and build a free-standing outdoor enclosure or gazebo. Patterned after free-flight aviaries, these enclosures contain the same kinds of enrichment. Dwarf fruit trees, platforms, and bedding vegetation provide all the freedom and enjoyment your Maine coon cat needs without the danger of traffic and other animals. A hammock could fit in there, too, but you'll have to share. For ideas and plans for designing and creating a room with a view for your cat, refer to periodicals on home improvement, building and supply stores, bookstores, and libraries. The MCBFA can send you the reprint "How to Construct an Outdoor Cat Run" by Connie Condit. Send $2 and a self-addressed envelope to Carol Downs, 57302 Peggy Drive, South Bend, Indiana 46619. Be sure to look in cat fancier magazines and bird fancier magazines. Some of the walk-in aviaries advertised in the latter could be adapted for feline use.

Cat Carriers

There are going to be some times when it will be necessary to take your Maine coon in a car even if it's only once a year to go to the veterinarian's for an annual examination and vaccinations. The basic cat carrier should: be rigid to afford some protection in case of an accident; be of large enough size to comfortably contain your Maine coon; have a simple-to-operate latch; be easy to clean; and be indestructible to the average cat. You should invest in a sturdy, plastic carrier with a hinged, latching door or lid for regular use. A decent size carrier costs less than $15 on sale at a discount store, and because you can expect to have your friend for 15 or more years, the carrier will be worth the investment.

My tip: Cardboard boxes and carriers are satisfactory in a pinch, but they are not ideal. Cardboard is not easy to clean; if your cat vomits or eliminates inside the carrier, the fluids will be absorbed by the cardboard leaving lingering odors and stains and will destroy it. Cardboard boxes and

A good compromise between allowing your Maine coon outdoors and keeping it indoors is giving it free access to a screened-in porch or deck. Add a climbing tree and some toys, and your cat should be quite content.

carriers do not have a good latching or closing mechanism and many cats easily devise an escape. I do not recommend soft "gym bag" style carriers either. They are easier to carry but do not provide any protection from impact in an accident.

If your Maine coon cat is injured and would otherwise be in pain if placed into its carrier, alternative transport can and should be used. Here's where cardboard boxes and carriers have an advantage because they're usually "top loading." Laundry or picnic baskets, drawers, dishpans, or any other rigid, open top household item can serve as an emergency carrier.

Important note: Do you have an emergency evacuation plan for your family in case of fire, flood, earth-

Cats love to be inside things. This Maine coon kitten is enjoying a carpet teepee.

A room with a view and all the accoutrements.

quake, or other natural disaster? Be sure to include evacuation of your Maine coon cat and other pets in your plan. Keep your cat's carrier assembled and in an easy-to-locate place in your home in case of emergency. Make sure that everyone knows where the carrier is kept.

Health Records

When you purchase your Maine coon kitten, ask the breeder to provide you with the dates of when the kitten received examinations and immunizations and bring this information with you to your veterinarian. Your new kitten should be examined by a veterinarian shortly after purchase, within 48 hours or two business days, according to MCBFA guidelines. Refer to your purchase agreement for the exact time frame. If your veterinarian detects a health problem, a reputable breeder will assume responsibility for all medical expenses involved in treatment or allow you to return the kitten according to the terms of the health guarantee in your purchase agreement.

At the time of your kitten or cat's first examination, your veterinarian will advise you as to what additional inoculations your new friend should receive and when your pet should receive them. Record and maintain this record of examinations, vaccinations, and treatments for the life of your Maine coon cat. Veterinarians can give you a health record folder to make this task easier. Also make note of any serologic test results and surgeries. If you really want to be thorough, peel the label off any empty medication bottles before you discard them, and stick them on an index card with a note as to indicated treatment, and slip the card in the pocket of the health record. Alternatively, you can use a spiral notebook.

Health records are especially important if you have more than one

Whether going on a five-minute jaunt to the veterinarian or a week-long tour of the countryside, your Maine coon will be safer in a carrier than loose in the back seat. Choosing a carrier should not be difficult because the selection is wide.

pet, because its awfully hard to keep track of who had what ailment as the years go by. Even though most veterinarians send reminder cards to their clients when their pets are due for vaccinations, you should know about when the vaccines are due on your own. Sometimes these cards are lost by a computer glitch or in the mail, or aren't forwarded by the post office if you move.

If you do move, ask your veterinarian for a photocopy of your Maine coon cat's medical record. The old record will help your new veterinarian become informed about your cat's past medical history and will prevent a lapse in important preventative health care.

Travel across some state and all national boundaries requires that you have a health certificate that declares your cat to be free of infectious diseases and lawfully inoculated against rabies. All airlines require this paperwork at the time of boarding. Health certificates are issued by your veterinarian. To obtain one, make an appointment for a physical examination. Bring your rabies certificate with you if the veterinarian issuing the health certificate is not the same one who administered the vaccine.

Things to Include in Your Maine Coon Cat's Health Record

Some of the information that you should have available to you in your personal records for your Maine coon cat include its medical record and several good photographs of your cat to be used for identification if your pet is ever lost. A photograph can be attached to a lost/found notice, photocopied, and posted in public places. Some owners make photograph postcards of lost pets and send them to veterinarians and animal shelters.

Include these items in your cat's health record:
• photographs
• vaccination history
• rabies certificates
• health certificates
• copies of medical records from previous veterinary
• hospitals or receipts for services
• breeder's name and address
• pedigree
• FeLV and FIV test results
• results of stool analysis for parasites
• your Maine coon cat's normal body weight

Basic Care

Introduction to the Home

The first few days at home with your new Maine coon kitten will be exciting for both of you. If it is at all possible, try to arrange for your new kitten to come home during a time when you can be there too. This will be your kitten's first time away from its mother and littermates and it may be frightened or lonely.

You can make this transition easier for your pet by being there to talk softly and handle it gently while it makes its exploration. Children should be made aware of the kitten's fear too, and be encouraged to play quietly with it. A timid kitten will quickly learn to keep away from loud and rambunctious children, a behavior that may persist as the kitten becomes an adult. Maine coon kittens from catteries that emphasize socialization should not be timid, and within a day or so should be boldly in control of the entire household.

The same suggestions apply to introducing an older kitten or adult Maine coon cat into your family. The difference in this situation is that older kittens and cats come to you with more knowledge of the behavior of humans and other strangers. Their response to voices, movement, and touch will depend a lot on past experience.

Regardless of age, the newest member of your family should be introduced to a limited area in your house at first. This is especially true for a kitten whose world is a much larger place. Food, water, and a litter box should be easily accessible in one or two rooms. With the litter box as a starting point, allow your kitten to explore. After ten or 15 minutes, put its back in the box to remind it where it is and allow your pet to continue to explore. Repeat these steps several times. Your kitten should remain confined to a limited area of the house until it has successfully located and used its litter box. This may take a few hours but after correctly finding the proper toileting area once, most kittens will faithfully return. Once your new cat or kitten has found its litter box, it is appropriate to broaden its horizons and allow your pet access to the rest of the house, room by room over several days. If your new kitten has litter box accidents, this usually means it is "forgetting" where the box is, so return to limiting your pet to a smaller area of the house.

You don't need to offer your kitten toys or other playthings right away. Your Maine coon kitten will get plenty of brain stimulation simply through exploration of its new environment. After a few days of adjustment, your pet will be ready for more interactive playthings.

After about an hour or so in its new home, you may offer your kitten food and water. Even if you have decided on a different kitten food for your new friend, you should feed it the same diet it has been fed up until your adoption. Once your kitten has become accustomed to its new home, you can begin to gradually switch its food by mixing the new diet in with the old one. Dietary changes can cause transient bouts of diarrhea, so until your pet is trained to the location of the litter box, it's best not to upset the applecart. (See Inappropriate

Exploring the great outdoors can be fun, but staying indoors is healthier. Maine coons that are allowed to roam outdoors are more susceptible to infectious diseases, parasites, accidents . . . and getting stuck in trees!

Elimination, page 60.) Always have fresh water available.

Going Outside

Your breeder has probably already discussed this issue with you and you may have signed a purchase agreement to limit your Maine coon kitten to the indoors. If you have agreed to this policy, you should abide by it but ultimately the choice is yours. Although going outdoors opens up a whole new world of exploits, it is fraught with dangers as well. Outdoor cats usually live shorter lives. They are more likely to be killed by moving vehicles or in other accidents. They are exposed to more infectious diseases, especially feline leukemia virus and feline infectious peritonitis, and despite vaccination they may contract these diseases. Outdoor cats have more gastrointestinal upsets and parasite infestation from hunting. And environmental stress like cold weather and rain take a toll, too.

Indoor-only cats can have just as rich a life as cats that go outdoors. Because they are not out roaming, indoor cats are free from the dangers of accidents and infections from fighting with other cats or wild animals. Accidental breeding and the birth of unwanted kittens are avoided. Proper diet and exercise will prevent boredom and obesity. And, indoor-only cats are rarely plagued by fleas!

If you choose to allow your Maine coon kitten to go outdoors, it should go out only with supervision until 14 to 16 weeks of age. Your pet should have completed all vaccine series for infectious diseases including the respiratory viruses, panleukopenia, feline leukemia virus, and especially rabies. Cats that are allowed to go outdoors should be neutered in a timely manner. Female cats should be spayed promptly at six months of age. Remember that there are no external signs of estrus or heat in female cats and that the behavioral signs may be absent or subtle at first. Your female cat can become pregnant during her first heat, as early as six or seven months of age. Male cats should be neutered when they are six to eight months old, and before the roaming, fighting, and urine spraying behaviors become established.

Identify Your Cat!

Outdoor venturing kittens and cats should be fitted with some form of identification such as a collar and name tag. The collar should have a piece of elastic that allows it to stretch over the head in case it becomes caught on something. Place the collar on your Maine coon kitten when it is young so that it gets used to wearing such identification. That way your pet will be less inclined to intentionally lose the collar while outside!

Some communities have the equipment for microchip identification of pets. A tiny capsule containing a microchip with a number is inserted under the skin, usually between the shoulder blades, using a special needle. The number is unique for each pet and is kept in a registry. The microchip number can be read using a handheld scanner over the shoulders. Lost pets can then be reunited with their owners by tracing the number. This identification method eliminates the problems associated with lost tags. Contact your city or town hall or your veterinarian about the availability of microchip identification in your community.

Moving to a New Neighborhood

If you relocate to a new home, plan to confine your Maine coon cat indoors for two to three weeks. By then, most of the boxes should be unpacked and your pet will have had time to become acquainted with the new place. Your cat's first ventures outdoors should be supervised by you, and your pet should wear some form of identification in case of exploring. If your cat leaves for an extended period of time, consider searching for your pet at your old home, especially if your move was a local one. Many, many cats will return to their old neighborhood.

Household Hazards

There are a few hazards of which you should be aware. Knitting, sewing, weaving supplies, and other stringlike materials should be safely stored away. Your Maine coon kitten or cat may consume linear objects that can cause obstruction and perforation of the gastrointestinal tract. Open containers of water including aquariums and toilet bowls should be closed to prevent the curious from drowning. Windows should be fitted with tight-fitting screens. This is especially important in high-rise buildings where many cats have attempted to snag perching

Kittens should go outdoors, if allowed to do so at all, only with supervision until 14 to 16 weeks old.

pigeons and have fallen many stories. Take an inventory of your household and landscaping plants and identify any that may be toxic if consumed by pets. If you are unsure of a plant's identification, a florist or garden shop may help you, or contact the National Animal Poison Control Center (see Useful Addresses and Literature, page 108).

Other potential hazards around the home include cleaning products and pharmaceuticals. Although your Maine coon cat is not likely to willingly drink many products if spilled, your pet may be inadvertently poisoned through accidental exposure such as by cleaning its paws after walking through spills. Bleach, iodine-based or pine oil-based cleaners are all very toxic to

An identification tag is a necessity for Maine coons that venture outside.

matter. Medical decisions are based on species specific knowledge.

A few pesticides and herbicides are potentially a problem around the home. Your Maine coon cat can be exposed through direct contact or by ingesting a chemically treated plant. Rodent poisons contain warfarin and other similar chemicals that cause fatal hemorrhage in animals that consume either the chemical directly, or the rodents that have been poisoned. Some of the newer rodenticides contain high levels of vitamin D-like substances that can result in kidney failure if consumed. When using these products around the home, always follow label instructions and keep track of where and when baits are placed. Molluscicides (snail baits) are occasionally consumed by cats and can cause neurologic signs like trembling and seizures. Similar signs are seen with inappropriate use of insecticides, including flea-control products.

Grooming

Your Maine coon cat is endowed with a luxurious and yet low-maintenance hair coat. Your pet will do most of the grooming by itself but to remain tangle-free, it will need some help from you. Grooming your Maine coon cat has other benefits for both of you as well. Grooming can be very relaxing as well as a time for special bonding and attention. Regular grooming alerts you early on to any skin problems, lumps, bumps, or fleas. It can help your Maine coon cat become accustomed to being handled. By removing loose fur, you help to reduce the incidence of vomiting from hair balls.

Mats are clumps of the downy undercoat that have been shed from hair follicles and trapped in the longer guard hairs. Maine coon cats do not have as dense an undercoat as Persian cats and some other long-haired breeds of cats, and so do not mat as severely or

cats and other pets. Inadequate rinsing of these chemicals from litter boxes or other surfaces may result in exposure. Your Maine coon cat should never be allowed to drink from a toilet, regardless of whether or not you use tank cleaners.

Aspirin, acetaminophen, ibuprofen, naproxen sodium, Pepto-Bismol and a few other common over-the-counter drug preparations may be found in the home. You should *never* give any of these or any other medication to your Maine coon cat unless specifically instructed to do so by your veterinarian. Old antibiotic prescriptions, human or veterinary, may be inappropriate in dosage, expired in potency, or just plain toxic to your Maine coon cat. Always seek assistance from a veterinary medical doctor in case of illness or accident. Your next-door neighbor may just happen to be a pediatrician, but cats are not small children in fur coats or dogs for that easily. Matting will occur during a heavy shed, or if a Maine coon cat fails to groom itself properly during illness or with age. Obese cats also have difficulty grooming themselves properly because they can't "reach."

During the spring and summer months, you should comb your Maine coon cat every one to three days depending upon the degree of shedding. In the fall and winter, you should only need to comb your pet once a week or so. Begin the grooming with a metal comb to loosen and remove "dead" hair and undercoat. Actually, all hair is "dead," but the shaft is lost from the hair follicle when it loosens during the senescent stage of hair growth. Comb your pet from the top of the head and over the neck and along the chest. Continue combing your Maine coon's ruff and shoulders; touching in these spots is usually well tolerated. By instituting grooming at an early age, you will desensitize your Maine coon kitten to combing along the lower back, tail base, tail, and flanks. Most mats, if they develop, do so on the underside of your Maine coon, especially under the forelegs. Underbelly combing is tolerated to various degrees by cats, but many kittens look at this as playtime and will initiate aggressive play behavior. You may get away with only a few passes with the comb at first until your cat is desensitized. Small mats can be removed by pulling with your fingers; apply gentle traction and they come free from the coat.

For larger mats, use a stitch ripper, or seam ripper (available in fabric stores and sewing departments) to slice them into smaller sections. Hold the mat at its base next to the skin and insert the blade of the stitch ripper into it and pull outward, away from the cat. Apply countertension with your fingers to prevent pulling on the skin. The smaller sections of mats can now be pulled free

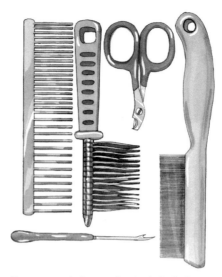

Recommended grooming tools include a metal comb, dematting comb, flea comb, stitch ripper, and nail trimmer.

with a comb. Some of the healthy hair will be damaged by this method, but it is less painful than pulling and tugging to free large mats en masse, and the coat will look less hacked than if you clip or shave them out.

If the matting is extensive, have a groomer remove the mats with a professional clipper rather than try to cut the mats out with scissors. Lacerations are a common occurrence when owners use scissors to trim out mats. It can be very difficult to see the mat against your Maine coon cat's light skin and you may easily misjudge where to cut.

If your Maine coon cat goes outdoors or if you have other pets that do, peel the fur out of the comb and inspect it closely for fleas or flea excrement or "dirt." Flea dirt appears as tiny black flecks or curved particles that fall freely from the fur. This is actually dried blood sucked from your cat and excreted as waste by the flea.

Maine coon cats do most of their own grooming. Here, a red mackerel kitten washes its foot.

If you sprinkle these particles onto wet paper and then streak the particles with your finger, reddish brown streaks appear confirming the presence of blood. You may not see live fleas on your Maine coon cat, but flea dirt means they've been there!

Bathing

Unless you plan to show your Maine coon cat, bathing will not be a necessary part of your grooming ritual. In fact, frequent bathing, especially with the wrong shampoo, can be damaging to your cat's skin and lovely hair coat. For general grooming, use a product formulated specifically for cats. Pet retail centers, catalogs, cat shows, and veterinary hospitals are the best places to find good products. Your breeder may recommend a favorite shampoo.

For skin infections, fleas, or other dermatopathies (skin disorders), use the product prescribed or recommended by your veterinarian and always follow label instructions as to proper application. Many products require a specific contact time with the coat for optimum performance. In this case, set a timer to be sure your cat is lathered long enough!

Before you begin a bath, gather all the necessary supplies, including an assistant if you're a novice and unsure about how your Maine coon cat will tolerate the water. You will need cotton for its ears to prevent water from entering the canals and neutral eye ointment to keep soapy water from irritating its eyes. Shampoo, towels, metal comb, and a blow dryer should be within reach. A spray attachment on the faucet is best for rinsing, but a small saucepan or bowl will also work.

Wet your cat's coat from head to tail, then lather it up in the same direction. Rinse the soap off thoroughly paying particular attention to under the legs. Gently squeeze out the excess water from the coat and towel dry. Remove the cotton from the ears. Blow-dry your friend with the dryer setting on low heat only. Use rubbing alcohol or witch hazel on a piece of cotton to absorb any water from its ears.

An alternative to wet bathing your Maine coon cat is dry bathing with fuller's earth, a coarse diatomaceous material available at some drugstores and at cat shows. Sprinkled into the coat, fuller's earth absorbs oils, then falls out or can be combed out of the fur. Cornstarch and other powders can also be used, but they can leave the coat appearing gray for several days.

Grooming for show is more meticulous and specialized. If you plan to show your Maine coon cat, talk to several breeders about the most current trends in show grooming. Judges like to see a long-haired cat's coat "float" through the air during judging, and breeders can tell you the latest and greatest tricks to achieving the favored look.

Nail Trimming

Every few weeks, trim the tips of the claws off with a trimmer. Trimming your Maine coon cat's nails is not very difficult to do, but you should start doing this when your pet is young so it gets used to the procedure, or as used to nail trimming as a cat can get! Kittens are easier to control for this grooming necessity and often need trimming the most. Those pinpoint sharp claws definitely grab your attention as the kitten climbs up your leg in an ambush or during rough play. You will probably need an assistant to scruff or stretch your cat by holding onto the loose skin over the back of its neck to get it to cooperate for a nail trim. If you are not comfortable doing this procedure at home, have your veterinarian show you how to do this when you are at the hospital.

There are several different types of commercial nail clippers for animals. They can be purchased for less than $10 at a pet supply store or at your veterinarian's office; choose the one you like the best. Some nail trimmers have a replaceable blade. Replace the blade or the trimmer whenever it becomes dulled with use. If the blade is dull, the end of the nail will appear ragged rather than smooth when cut. A pair of folding human finger nail or toenail trimmers works very well for kittens and most adult cats.

Hold one toe over the last joint between your thumb and forefinger. If you squeeze the joint gently, the claw flexes outwardly. Clip off the sharp tip, avoiding the pink center called the quick, which bleeds if the nail is cut too short. Repeat for each claw.

Note: If you do cut a claw too short, stop the bleeding by applying continuous pressure to the end of the nail for about a minute (no peeking.) Styptic powder (Kwik-Stop) or silver nitrate applicator sticks are chemical cauterizers and are available at pet stores.

Grooming can be a special time for Maine coon and owner. It brings relaxation, bonding, and welcome attention.

They work very well and are handy to have around, but they do cause a burning sensation to the toe and the silver nitrate can stain your fingers or counter tops. A dab of flour or an ice cube held on the end of the nail is also effective for controlling this hemorrhage.

Be on the alert for ingrown claws. In very old cats that don't take care of themselves, the old nail sheath tends to be retained over the new nail as it is growing in. These old sheaths can be pushed into the toe pads causing an infection. When you trim the nails of an old cat's claws, you'll notice that you have to peel away the remnants of the old nail to see a tiny new one beneath it. If you discover an embedded nail, pain, a foul odor, or a discharge from your Maine coon cat's toes, have your cat examined and the nails trimmed by your veterinarian.

49

HOW-TO: Controlling Fleas

Let's look at the flea life cycle. Of the fleas that parasitize dogs and cats, the adult fleas live their lives on the animal. The adult female feeds by sucking blood, then mates and lays eggs on your Maine coon cat. Blood is the sole food source for the adult flea, and because the female flea is laying enormous numbers of eggs, she is feeding frequently. The blood meal is digested and then excreted as flea feces, which look like little specks of black pepper in your Maine coon cat's coat. This is sometimes the only evidence that you find of a flea infestation.

The flea eggs and feces fall freely off of your Maine coon's coat. Out of the eggs hatch tiny, translucent larvae that you can also see in areas where your cat spends a lot of time sleeping, if you look closely enough. The larvae feed on the flea feces as well as skin scales and other organic debris. Flea larvae will not survive in dry climates where there is a relative humidity of less than 50 percent. But even in dry climates, deep between carpet fibers and shaded areas of the lawn and under bushes, there are microenvironments that support the larvae.

Flea larvae spin a sticky cocoon and enter a pupa stage. This stage can last for a few days up to several months. If conditions are right, the pupae hatch and out comes a new adult flea seeking a host from which to suck a blood meal. This newly hatched adult must find another suitable host within three or four days or it will die. The pupae will continue to lie dormant if there is no host, i.e., a cat or other animal, including humans, around for the next stage to feed on. These pupae can lie dormant for many months. The pupae are stimulated to hatch by carbon dioxide breathed off by the host and from the vibrations of footsteps or, as luck would have it, from the vacuum cleaner!

To effectively control fleas, you must attack them at every part of the life cycle. To take the easy route and simply apply a flea collar or give a weekly bath, will doom you to failure. Unless you live in a climate that does not support fleas, managing rather than eliminating a flea problem is the best you can do.

A program for total flea control involves treating the cat and the environment. Although flea baths have a quick-kill effectiveness and can eliminate adult fleas on your cat, flea baths have no residual effect. Once the soap is washed off, the newly hatched adults will jump right back on. Residual flea control on the cat means using an insecticidal spray, powder, dip, collar, or foam after the cat is bathed.

Flea combs have special teeth that trap fleas as they run through the fur. It is possible to mechanically remove the fleas using a flea comb and thereby not use an insecticide directly on the cat. In households with a small flea-control problem, this approach may be feasible for removing most but probably not all of the adult fleas. Because fleas move between the hair shafts with ease and agility, and because the newly hatched adults are small, some fleas will escape the comb and go on to feed, lay eggs, and defecate dried blood. If you decide to use a flea comb to control adult fleas on your Maine coon cat, you should still treat the environment.

Note: Keep in mind that all the pets in the household must be involved in your flea-control program.

Insect growth regulators are hormones that cause the flea eggs to dry up and not hatch. They work only on fleas, not on animals (including the people

A flea bath eliminates the adult fleas on an animal. Follow up a bath with residual flea control, such as an insecticidal spray, powder, dip, or foam, or a flea collar, to discourage newly hatched fleas from staying on your pet and new fleas from jumping onboard.

that handle them). Although insecticides are still the backbone of all flea programs, they fail to kill the eggs. Insect growth regulators essentially render the fleas sterile and break the flea life cycle. It is only by breaking this life cycle that fleas can effectively be controlled. Insect growth regulators have been incorporated into both on-the-animal and premise flea-control products and soon they will be available in an oral form.

Boric acid compounds are a second alternative to environmental insecticides. Applied to the environment, boric acid reduces the humidity in the microenvironment (i.e., the carpet) of the flea, making it very unfavorable for the flea larvae's survival. Unfortunately, simply sprinkling boric acid powder around doesn't work very well. It must be manufactured and applied properly to be effective. There are a few boric acid derivative flea-control products for the premises that you can purchase, and there are some professional flea-control companies that specialize in this service. These are ideal for anyone who needs to avoid even the safest of environmental insecticides.

Environmental control means using insecticides and insect growth regulators in areas where your Maine coon spends most of its time: in the house and in parts of the yard. Room foggers or aerosol or pump sprays should be used in your cat's favorite rooms, under and on the furniture where it sleeps, and along hallways where it walks. You may not need to apply these products to every room. For instance, if your

A flea comb's tightly spaced teeth trap fleas running through a cat's fur. Hot spots on a Maine coon that should get special combing attention are the base of the tail, the belly, and the neck.

cat is not allowed in a guest bedroom, it is unlikely that there would be any flea eggs or larvae there. However, keep in mind that in heavily infested households, fleas can jump onto your clothing and be transported into areas where you go and your Maine coon cat doesn't. You can even bring fleas home from a friend's house that way!

Likewise, it is also important to treat certain areas of your yard in those cool, damp places where your Maine coon likes to spend the most time. This is an important reservoir for fleas often overlooked by owners.

You should treat the environment at least twice, because the pupae are resistant to all chemicals, about three weeks apart. The first treatment should kill most of the adults, larvae, and eggs. The subsequent treatment will kill the newly emerged adults. After the initial set of envi-

ronmental treatments, you will need to maintain your control by periodically retreating the environment, and regularly applying a spray, powder, or foam to your cat. Failure of any flea-control program is usually due to use of ineffective products, incorrect application, inappropriate timing of applications, or failure to treat an area of the environment serving as a reservoir for flea eggs, larvae, and pupae.

The natural methods of flea control using herbs, garlic, nutritional yeast, or other sources of B vitamins, ultrasonic flea collars, and boxes do not work—no matter how hard you wish they would, even if your very best and trusted friend swore by this method. All insecticides are not heinous and lethal. Some, such as the pyrethrins derived from a certain species of chrysanthemum, are natural botanicals, and are highly effective at killing fleas quickly. Your veterinarian can give you up-to-date information about specific brands of flea-control products.

Safety and effectiveness also depend upon proper application and use of flea products. Manufacturers of the products have detailed instructions for entire flea-control programs that include instructions for each step and product. Some programs have a toll-free telephone number for technical services. You can call and discuss your specific circumstances with a trained technician who will know more about the products you are using and how to get the most from the program.

Grooming can also be considered preventative medicine. Skin problems, lumps, bumps, and fleas can be detected early, and loose fur can be removed before it ends up as a hair ball.

A Word About Declawing

Regularly scheduled nail trims along with proper scratching-post training will save your furniture and drapery from damage. When nail trimming and training fail, there are several alternatives: nail caps, deep digital flexor tendonectomy, and declawing.

Many cat owners are quick to elect surgical declawing at the first sign of claw damage in the home. Keep in mind that many Maine coon breeders have a "claw clause" in their purchase contract that forbids surgical declawing. And for good reason. Surgical declawing is an amputation procedure that changes the weight-bearing surface of the paw and inflicts at least temporary and potentially long-term pain. Anecdotally, many agree that cats that have been declawed are more quick to bite when threatened. A declawed Maine coon cat cannot be shown in a Cat Fanciers' Association show ring and can only be shown in the Household Pet Class with The International Cat Association. The great majority of cats tolerate nail trimming and can be trained to use a scratching post of some sort. Surgical declawing should be reserved for the few exceptions where this fails. If you are considering declawing your Maine coon cat, you owe it to your pet to fully educate yourself about this and other alternative procedures.

Nail caps are a relatively new product available to cat owners who cannot get their cat's nails trimmed short enough to prevent damage to furniture and flesh. They are available through veterinarians who will apply them to your cat's nails on the first go-around and show you how to reapply them at home if you wish, but many people prefer that their veterinarians perform this task for them. Nail caps are soft, molded, plastic sheaths with blunted tips that slide over the nail. They are held on using an adhesive similar to that used for women's artificial nails. Nail caps usually remain in place for about four weeks until they become dislodged or are shed along with the cat's own nail sheath. At that time, the capped nails are trimmed back and the old caps are removed and replaced by a new set. Nail caps come in a variety of sizes for different ages of cat, and a variety of fashion colors for different owners.

Nail capping has benefits and disadvantages. Even neatly trimmed claws can still injure someone with fragile skin, such as infants and the elderly. Nail caps can protect the skin from injury. Nail capping is arguably more humane than the other alternatives for controlling damage done by a cat's scratching. It is not a surgical procedure and can be performed during a routine office visit to your veterinarian. Cats do not need to be sedated or anesthetized to have nail capping. It is technically not a difficult procedure, so owners can master it at home if they choose. And most cats seem to tolerate the caps over their claws.

On the other hand, nail capping has not been available for very long, so there hasn't been experience with a large number of cats that have worn them for a long time. Therefore, it is not known what the long-term effects will be for a cat that wears nail caps. Long-term effects could include nail bed infections or hypersensitivity reactions to the glue or plastic. Because the caps only last about a month, they will need frequent replacement, which over the long run will be more expensive than other alternatives. Many owners become tired of having to replace the caps so frequently and abandon their use or choose another method of controlling the scratching. Nail capping does require two people to get the job done without gluing the caps to your own fingers or having the cat escape and run around half-capped.

Flexor tendonectomy is another method of controlling the damage done by scratching. This is a surgical procedure and will require general anesthesia. Flexor tendonectomies are not widely performed by veterinarians, so you may have to ask several if they are familiar with the technique.

Briefly, tendonectomy involves removing a small (2- or 3-millimeter) section of the tendon that allows the cat to flex its claws through a very small incision on the bottom of each toe, just behind the pad. By cutting the tendon and removing a small piece, the cat can no longer flex its claws. Other than the tendon, the toes and claws are left intact, and the cat walks normally on the foot. Recovery from the surgery is rapid and there seems to be much less discomfort than after a traditional declaw. Because hemorrhage is not a problem, tendonectomy patients can go home the same day

A Maine coon's long hair should "float" through the air during a show to satisfy the judges.

as their surgery. This procedure is particularly good for mature cats or obese cats that have longer recoveries and more discomfort after declawing than kittens and young cats.

Tendonectomy has its disadvantages, too. Right away, you may have difficulty finding a veterinarian who is familiar with the technique. Tendonectomy is not suitable for any cat that has any ongoing medical problems with its toes, such as dermatitis that involves the feet and pads. Because the cat can no longer dig its claws into surfaces, it cannot remove the outer nail sheath that is being shed. You must trim the claws of a tendonectomized cat in order to remove these sheaths. As the new nail grows in, the old sheath will be pushed forward and around toward the pad. An infection can occur if it becomes embedded in the pad. Fortunately, nail trimming is usually only needed about every two or three months.

Declawing is a fourth method for controlling scratching damage in cats and is very controversial. Declawing is also a surgical procedure that requires general anesthesia and one or two days of hospitalization. Declawing involves amputation of the end of the cat's toe. Declawing your Maine coon cat will be equivalent to amputation of

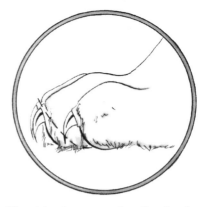

When trimming your pet's nails, clip off the sharp tip. Be careful to avoid the pink center, which is called the quick and bleeds if the nail is cut too short.

Trim your Maine coon's nails every few weeks. Have an assistant hold your pet by the scruff of the neck while you clip off the claw tips.

the tips of your fingers at the joint just above your fingernails.

This amputation changes the weight-bearing surface of the cat's paws. The claw is removed in its entirety along with the bone and the growth plate from which the claw emerges. The amputation is done either with a guillotine-type instrument or by dissection. The defect in the toe is then closed with a single absorbable suture or liquid tissue adhesive. Some veterinarians choose not to close the defect, although the healed paw is more cosmetically pleasing if the defect is closed. Because there is considerable hemorrhage associated with this surgery, light pressure bandages are applied for several hours afterward, and the cat must remain in the hospital one or more days to prevent further bleeding once the bandages are removed.

Declawing can be performed as young as 12 weeks of age and, in fact, young kittens tolerate this procedure extremely well. Recovery time is quite rapid and there seems to be little discomfort. Recovery time and pain are longer and more significant in older or heavier cats. Occasionally a claw will grow back and will need to be removed again. In either case, after tendonectomy or declawing, shredded or pelleted newspaper litter should be used in the litter box for at least a week after surgery. These cats should remain indoors during this time. These precautions are taken to prevent infection.

Despite the rumors to the contrary, tendonectomized and declawed cats can defend themselves quite effectively. The front claws of a cat are used primarily for warning swipes at their offenders. The real defense lies in the back claws and teeth. A cat in combat will hug its opponent tightly with its forelegs and strike and bite repeatedly with its canine teeth all the while raking with its rear claws. Tendonectomized and declawed cats can climb trees, too. However, it should be very obvious that cats that have been declawed on all four feet should never be allowed outside, as they are indeed defensively handicapped.

Traveling with Your Maine Coon Cat

Vacations, relocation to a new home, or trips to the veterinarian, groomer, or boarding kennel are some of the possible times when you will be traveling with your cat. Some of this travel will be unavoidable, especially trips to the veterinary hospital unless you have a mobile veterinarian come to your home. Moving your cat to a new home means you'll need to do a little more planning than what you'll already be doing for yourself and your belongings. But for vacation travel, you have other options.

Always include a harness and a leash among your Maine coon's luggage when traveling out of town.

Should I Bring My Maine Coon Cat with Me on Vacation?

Vacation trips pose predictable problems for pet owners. Should you bring your cat along, or would it be happier and safer if left at home? Certainly for short absences like weekend get-aways, your cat can get along just fine if left alone with an adequate supply of dry food and water and a clean litter box.

During longer absences, you'll need to consider either bringing your pet with you or providing some type of care. What will be your accommodations at your destination? Will your cat be a welcome guest to your friends? Does the hotel allow pets and with what special arrangements? There are several publications available that list major hotel chains that accept well-behaved pets. Some require a security deposit and may restrict you to certain (smoking) rooms. Will your cat be left alone for long periods of time while you are sightseeing or vacationing? If you are camping or staying in a cabin, do you expect your cat to stay around this temporary homestead? I've met a few cats that have spent several weeks each winter and summer at the same "camp." The people ski, fish, and canoe while the cat communes with the local wildlife.

How tolerant is your cat to strangers and strange environments? If there is any question that your cat may become lost or stressed by vacationing with you, please leave it at home in the care of capable friends, or in a boarding kennel that accommodates cats. If you think that travel will be rewarding for both of you, by all means plan well and enjoy yourselves.

Ground Travel

Traveling with your cat requires special considerations. How well does your cat tolerate the car? Cats that travel regularly, starting in kittenhood, are usually tolerant of the motion and noise. Even if your cat hasn't had this opportunity, you can still get it used to the car by taking a few "practice" trips before your planned departure. Short trips can sometimes desensitize a cat to motion sickness by reducing the apprehension associated with travel. Travel across certain borders will require some health documentation: a rabies certificate and possibly a health certificate signed by a veterinarian.

Never leave your Maine coon cat in a car during the warmer months. The inside temperature may reach well over 100°F (37.8°C) in only a few minutes, and your pet may die. If you must stop, bring the carrier with you if possible. Plan shady picnics rather than restaurant lunches. And always have your cat on a harness and leash if you let it out of the car or carrier at rest stops.

Air and Rail Travel

If you're not traveling by auto but rather by airplane or train, you will need to consult the transportation carrier about specific requirements such as health documents, cat carriers, food, and water. Health documents must be obtained within a certain time frame of travel for them to be valid, and this will require a visit to your veterinarian.

Also inquire about where your cat will be put on the plane or train. Carriers have rules about animals traveling in passenger compartments. Most pets travel in the cargo compart-

When you stop during a long car trip to stretch your legs or enjoy a picnic lunch, let your Maine coon out of the car, too. But don't forget the harness and leash!

ment of an airplane. Just as your luggage may be lost, so may your kitty.

More About Cat Carriers

A cat carrier is an absolute necessity when your cat is traveling in the car. Most cats tolerate this, especially after they've been taken on a few car trips. Some cats yowl or otherwise vocalize; a few cats will try to scratch their way out of the box, and with some success if the carrier is a cardboard one.

Do not give in to your Maine coon cat's protestations! The yowling may be irritating and certainly pitiful, but for its safety, do not allow your Maine coon to roam freely within the vehicle. Most vocal cats will stop yowling after a few miles. It's not safe for your pet to be held in a passenger's arms or to sit next to you on the seat or in the

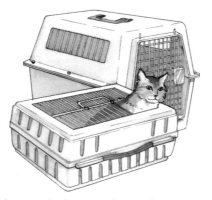

A cat carrier is a must for traveling away from home. An airline-approved model is best.

never, ever allow them free access to the inside of the car again, and we took many trips together cross-country after that. And I continue to plead with all my clients to put their cats in a carrier!

Tip: Some cats will vomit, urinate, or defecate from motion or stress during transport. Line the inside of the carrier with several layers of newspaper or a small towel. If your Maine coon cat is frantic about being inside the carrier, consider having your veterinarian make a house call for its annual examination. Although routine tranquilization is not a good idea, some very frantic cats or cats with severe motion sickness will benefit from the use of drugs.

rear window. A sudden stop or collision will send your pet careening about and possibly through the windshield. If the driver and passengers are seriously injured, it will be left to the emergency personnel to rescue the cat as well as the injured people. The medical technicians' first responsibility will be to the injured people; they may not even notice your cat and it could die. Your Maine coon could run from the accident and be lost, or someone could be seriously scratched or bitten trying to help it.

When I was a veterinary student, I would take one or two trips each year, back to my home in Connecticut with my cats. We would travel through the mountain tunnels of Pennsylvania along the turnpike and sometimes I would let my two cats Willie and Neige sit in the back window of my hatchback. On one trip, as we passed through one of those tunnels, the hatchback flew open. Had Willie and Neige been sitting in the window as they had done at other times they would have both been vacuumed right out of the car. The thought of having my cats ripped apart by the traffic following behind me was enough to

Other Travel Supplies

If you're going to be on the road for several days, disposable cardboard litter boxes are a big convenience. Disposable boxes are sold individually at supermarkets and pet supply stores and look like collapsible gift boxes. Bring a small amount of your cat's preferred litter with you. When you settle into your accommodations for the evening, set up the box with a handful of litter. Simply dispose of the box before you resume your travel. Don't worry about providing litter facilities in the car or carrier; your Maine coon cat won't miss them.

Also bring along a supply of your cat's regular food and bowls for feeding and watering. You don't need to provide food or water in the carrier. It may spill and your cat probably won't eat or drink anyway, so wait until you settle in for the night to offer food. You can offer your pet water during rest stops if you like, but don't be surprised if it isn't interested even though you may feel parched.

Important note: Although a health certificate may not be required, always bring proof of rabies vaccination with you when you travel out-of-state with your Maine coon cat.

Alternatives to Traveling with Your Maine Coon

If your travels require that your pet stay behind, three options are offered. Maine coon cats are mellow enough to be left at home with a daily visit by a friend or neighbor. If you don't have a friend who can help, contract a professional pet-sitter or house-sitter. Ask your veterinarian to recommend someone who provides this service.

If you'll feel more secure if your cat had 24-hour supervision, make arrangements with a boarding kennel. Some cater exclusively to cats. Be sure that you call well ahead of the time you anticipate needing to board. And always make an on-site inspection of a new facility before you commit to leaving your cat. Discuss all special feeding and care instructions with the director at the time you make reservations.

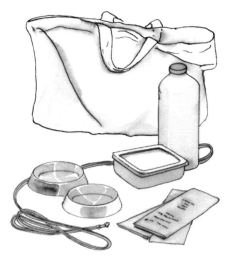

Travel supplies should include disposable litter boxes, a supply of litter, food and water bowls, health documents, a leash, and a bag to hold everything.

Behavior and Training

One breeder described the Maine coon cat temperament to me like this: If you put a box with an alligator in it on the floor, an "X" cat (the breed shall remain nameless) would jump right in. A Maine coon would look into the box, call over other Maine coon cats, and have a conference about it. Then they'd all jump in. I believe his point was that the Maine coon is an intelligent cat but lives with joy and a touch of reckless abandon. Most of what your Maine coon cat does will bring you joy and maybe a little exasperation.

Many behaviors that pet owners see as "bad" or "wrong" are often normal for a cat. A few of the more common problems that cat owners have confronted me with over the last 11 years may help you to correct a "wrong" behavior. Consult your veterinarian for help with specific concerns. Veterinary behaviorists are available for consultation regarding complex problems. *Before you try to correct a behavior problem, have your cat examined for medical causes of the behavior.*

Inappropriate Elimination

Inappropriate elimination behavior, or elimination in inappropriate locations, e.g., outside of the litter box, is the most common behavior problem for which owners seek advice. The elimination can include urination, defecation, or both, can occur at any age, and can be an extremely frustrating problem to solve. There are many inciting causes for inappropriate elimination, including changes in the brand, odor, or texture of the litter, inadequate cleaning of the litter box, inadequate number of boxes for the number of cats in the household, and lack of privacy. In multiple-cat households, one cat may "guard" the box and prevent other cats from using it. One cat may stalk and pounce on another as it leaves the box. Each of these factors may cause aversion and lead to elimination in inappropriate areas. Urinary tract disease, parasite infestation, bowel disorders, and diarrhea can cause inappropriate elimination, and medical conditions must be ruled out first before behavior modification is attempted.

The first step in correcting this problem is to clearly define it. You must answer the following questions:
- When did the behavior start?
- Where does the cat eliminate?
- Does the cat urinate, defecate, or both?
- Is the urine/feces normal in appearance?
- Does the problem occur at every elimination?
- Has this ever been a problem before?
- What recent changes have taken place in the household?
- Are there any changes to the litter box?
- Are there new kittens/cats in the household?

Be sure that you have followed the instructions regarding litter boxes and fillers (see page 30). Areas that have been used for elimination must be thoroughly cleaned and deodorized *to the cat's standards* to prevent the cat from returning to those spots. Sometimes it's necessary to start at the beginning and retrain a cat by confining your pet to a small room with the box. Make sure that you place the food and water dishes well away from the litter box. Do not allow the cat to have unsupervised access to the remainder of the house. After a few weeks of consistent litter box use, the cat can be introduced to other rooms, preferably one at a time.

A cat's aversion to urinating or defecating where it eats can be used to retrain it. Put a bowl of food at the spot where the cat eliminates. A piece of tinfoil or tape may also deter it. The opposite technique is to actually put another litter box over the spot and allow your cat to use it. After a few days, move the box a few inches at a time over to where you want it to be.

Some cats have a preference for elimination on certain surface textures, such as newspaper or carpeting, and will return repeatedly to those surfaces regardless of how well you clean and deodorize them. In this case, the only solution is to remove the surface, either pull up the carpet and replace with another textured surface, or do not permit the cat to come into this area.

Inappropriate elimination can be treated with medication, and this may make your retraining more effective. Drugs used alone are often ineffective.

Urine Spraying

Urine spraying is a completely normal behavior. It just happens to be unacceptable to humans and is therefore considered to be a "problem." In reality, more likely it is the cat that has the problem. In my experience, urine spraying occurs most often when a cat is experiencing the stress of too many cats in one household, seeing other cats outside the window, outside cats that spray windows or doors, and confinement to the indoors. Although less likely than with inappropriate elimination, urinary tract disorders can sometimes lead to spraying.

A Maine coon such as this brown classic tabby may look very elegant relaxing on a polished table in your living room, but scratches in the wood or broken knick knacks may be an unwanted result.

Both males and females spray urine in order to mark their territory. Urine spraying must be distinguished from inappropriate urination, because the plan for erasing these two behaviors is different. When a cat sprays urine, he (or she) does not squat low as when urinating but rather stands normally on all four legs or slightly on tiptoe in the rear with the tail erect. The tail quivers as the urine is released. Urine is usually sprayed on upright objects.

Unneutered male and female cats are most often the problem sprayers. Spraying can become a learned behavior too, so early neutering, before the behavior ever starts, is advised. Correcting the problem requires eliminating the inciting cause. This may mean reducing the number of cats in the household or blocking windows or doors so that indoor cats can't see the outdoor ones. In some instances, the strictly indoor cat must be allowed access to the outdoors by some means (see A Room with a View, page 38). Urine spraying has also been treated successfully with medication.

Scratching the Furniture

Scratching furniture is another normal cat behavior. Cats scratch in order to mark territory and to remove the old sheath from new claws. For this reason, scratching is an important behavior that prevents the new claw from pushing the old one around and into the pad. Cats have texture preferences for scratching, and the key to training your cat to use a scratching post instead of your couch is identifying that preference. The preference can be for cloth, leather, carpet, or wood. Within the cloth category, the texture can be loopy, velvety, rough, or smooth. Purchase a scratching post that meets your cat's specifications, or buy a fabric remnant and secure it to the post. If your pet likes wood, why not give it a log?

You may need to have more than one post, because placement is also important. If your cat likes to have a good stretch and scratch after a nap, put the post right next to its sleeping area. If your pet prefers to saunter over to your stereo speaker, put the post next to the speaker. You may see your Maine coon kitten scratching as part of its play behavior. When you see this happen, bring your cat over to the scratching post and rub its paws on the post. The earlier you start the training, the more successful you will be at teaching it the appropriate spot to do what's normal.

There are upright and corner-mounted posts, posts incorporated into cat trees and perches, and carpeted scratching pads that lie flat on the floor. The design should be stable; your cat won't use a post that falls over. Rub, sprinkle, or spray on a little catnip in order to attract your pet to the post. Because scratching is a marking behavior, your cat may be more attracted if you slip a piece of your clothing over it, such as a worn but unlaundered sweatshirt.

Aggressive Play

Some of the behaviors that may endear you to kittens can also be maddening. Oh it's just delightful when they race up the cat tree, but maybe not so nice when it's the drapery. Pouncing on a catnip mouse is good; pouncing on your head at 3 A.M. is not. Sinking teeth and claw into your ankle as you pass a doorway along the hall isn't so charming either.

These are all normal play behaviors that are seen between kittens in a litter. All of the pouncing, stalking, chasing, and boxing is done to one another, and continues to a degree until the kittens are old enough to disperse and live on their own. Normally the kittens keep each other in line and they learn just how rough to play. Play behaviors are an important part of learning to hunt and survive.

You may acquire kittens at the height of this play behavior. Unless you acquire more than one at a time,

Stop a kitten's roughhousing with remote punishment. Spritz it with water from a squirt bottle or a puff of air from a can of compressed air. Neither will hurt the kitten.

all this energy has to be diverted somewhere—it's the older cat, the dog, and usually the people who become the focus. Toys, paper bags, and other inanimate objects are fun, but your kitten wants to play with something that plays back and that's fine until things get out of hand or someone gets wounded.

When your kitten gets that glassy-eyed stare, turns its ears to the side, swings its head to-and-fro, and you get the feeling that you're looking like a giant mouse, it's time for a time-out. Put your kitten in a quiet room by itself for a few minutes and let it calm down. This may be the only solution for its nocturnal attacks to your feet. Cats are naturally active at night. Much as you may want your kitten to sleep with you, this may be impossible until it is a little older and has settled down.

Sometimes a time-out isn't enough to stop aggressive play behavior, and some type of indirect punishment is required. *Never, ever hit your kitten or cat.* Corporal punishment doesn't work with cats. Your kitten must be thwarted using remote punishment or aversion; your pet shouldn't know that it's coming from you.

Some types of remote punishment include a squirt from a squirt bottle, a puff from a can of compressed air (used to clean camera lenses), or a loud rattle of a soda can with a few coins. These things startle the kitten enough to stop the behavior. In a split second, you can stop and divert its attention. Note that these "punishments" do not hurt the kitten and are not directly associated with you. Use the most fleeting punishment necessary to affect the behavior.

Scat Cat!

Your Maine coon cat may look right at home sitting next to the crystal fruit bowl on your dining room table, but unless you want your pet to join the

Some well-placed sticky tape can teach an invading Maine coon where it is and is not allowed to go.

family at Thanksgiving dinner, perhaps you should give some thought to making some places off-limits. Certainly you can close off rooms where you don't want your cat to go—the guest room or dining room, for instance. The remote punishment techniques may be helpful to deter your Maine coon cat from going onto countertops and the like as long as you are at home and catch it in the act.

What about when you're not home? The best answer may be sticky tape, which was suggested to me by a friend who was a veteran of a four-cat household. Purchase a roll of wide, 2 to 3 inches (5–7.6 cm), clear packing tape and cut strips about 18 inches long (45.7 cm). Lay them with the sticky side up fairly close together on top of the counters or furniture on which you'd like to restrict your cat, and leave them there. This will make

Does anyone have a squirt bottle?

fact, the tape will stick for quite some time and remind your cat of its transgression, often until you get home, unless its clever enough to get the tape off itself. Very few encounters with the sticky tape are needed to discourage your cat from ever venturing onto the forbidden surfaces, but a refresher course is occasionally necessary.

A visit to your local electronics store can give you a few ideas on how to rig up remote punishment devices such as alarms or lights using a motion sensor to aid in training your cat to stay out of certain rooms or areas within the home.

Fighting and Roaming

Fighting and roaming are also normal cat behaviors. Cats do not respect property boundaries, yours or anyone else's. If you let your Maine coon cat outdoors, do not

working in these areas a little difficult for a few days, but now when you're not home and your cat jumps onto these surfaces, the tape will stick to its fur and your pet won't like that. In

Be careful where you place the litter box. Privacy is important, but the box should not be so out of the way that your kitten will not be able to find it or get into it. A misplaced litter box could cause elimination problems.

This blue mackerel tabby's bright, alert eyes and full, shiny coat are outward indicators of its excellent health, diet, environment, and care.

expect it to stay in the yard. This is simply contrary to the nature of the cat. If you want to eliminate the roaming, that's easy—just keep your Maine coon cat indoors.

Maine coon cats are widely known to be extremely tolerant of other cats and pets. Not all cats will get along, however, and occasionally you may have territorial battles even within the home. Territorial battles can be minimized or eliminated by neutering. Rarely it is necessary to keep some cats separated from one another.

Nutrition and Feeding

The Basics of Nutrition

The six major nutrients needed by your cat are carbohydrates, proteins, fats, vitamins, minerals, and, the most important one, water.

Three of the six major nutrients can be used by the body to produce a chemical energy needed to power life processes, and heat. The heat released when these nutrients are "burned" by the body is measured in Calories. Carbohydrates and proteins release approximately 4 kcals or Calories per gram weight. Fats contain more than twice as many Calories at 9 kcals per gram weight.

Carbohydrates come from plant sources: grains, seeds, vegetables, and grasses. Carbohydrates can be simple in their chemical structure, like sugar, or complex, like cellulose. Cellulose and other similar complex carbohydrates make up the physical structure of plants. Some of these complex carbohydrates cannot be digested by animals, and are then labeled dietary fiber. Although it is not digested, fiber plays an important role in normal intestinal function.

Proteins are made up of smaller chemical subunits linked together called amino acids. Proteins make up all the tissues and fluids of animals; they serve a structural role. Proteins also function as hormones and chemical transmitters within nerves. It is the sequence and arrangement of the amino acids in a protein that determine the function of that protein.

Proteins are derived from animal tissues; they are also available from plants. Once consumed by an animal, digestion breaks down protein into its constituent amino acids, then they are absorbed into circulation and reassembled into structural proteins needed by the animal. Animals can also make some amino acids on their own, but not all of them. Although there are 23 amino acids, cats require that 11 of them be provided by the diet. Twelve others can be synthesized in the body. Taurine is one amino acid that is required in the cat's diet, but not in the dog's. This amino acid is critical for normal heart function and vision. Arginine is another amino acid required in much higher amounts by cats. Arginine is essential for converting the waste product ammonia into urea, so that it can be excreted by the kidneys. Inadequate amounts of arginine in the diet can cause depression and seizures.

A cat must eat several different sources of protein in order to obtain all 11 of the essential amino acids. The proteins from meat contain a greater variety of amino acids than do proteins from plants. Amino acids are also burned for energy. In most healthy animals, dietary protein should be avoided in excess. The cat is unique among animals, however, because the cat is one species that actually requires that some of its dietary protein be used for energy as well as the synthesis of structural proteins needed within the body. The reason for this species difference is not known, but this is one reason why cats require more protein in their diet than dogs. And because of their additional requirement for the animal tissue-derived amino acid taurine, they are true obligate carnivores. This is an important point. Cats should not be fed dog food.

Fats serve several functions within the body. They are a highly efficient source of energy (9 kcals/gram). Fats are also necessary for the absorption of some vitamins: vitamins A, D, E, and K. They are also important in the formation of some hormones. Fats are similar to proteins in that they are made up of subunits called fatty acids. There are two essential fatty acids for the cat, that is, they are required to be taken in with the diet: linoleic and arachidonic.

Fats can be found in both vegetable matter and animal tissue. Liquid fats like safflower and corn oil consist of 50 to 70 percent linoleic acid. Only animal fats contain arachidonic acid, and it is a cat's requirement for arachidonic acid in the diet also makes it a truly carnivorous animal.

Vitamins can be divided into two groups: those that will dissolve in water and those that will dissolve in fat. Vitamins that dissolve in water are called water soluble, and these are the various B vitamins and vitamin C. Vitamins that dissolve in fat are called fat soluble. These include vitamins A, D, E, and K. Vitamins are used in the energy-producing reactions of the body. They are important in wound healing, tissue repair, maintaining healthy skin, hair coat, and bones, and blood clotting. Many animals, including dogs and people, can synthesize some vitamins; for example, vitamin A can be synthesized from beta-carotene, the substance that gives carrots their orange color. The B vitamin called niacin can be synthesized from biotin. This is not true, however, for cats. Cats require both vitamin A and niacin in their diet. These vitamins are found in animal tissues, and again, their requirement makes the cat a truly carnivorous animal. Because cats have different requirements for the levels of vitamins in their diet, they should not be fed dog food.

Vitamin deficiencies are rarely a problem in healthy cats eating a wholesome diet. Deficiencies could occur if a cat were to be fed a poorly formulated diet or one that was improperly stored or preserved. Vitamins are destroyed by the high temperatures used in cooking and processing of cat foods. This is most often the case with generic or very inexpensive cat foods and with home-cooked diets. Improperly processed fish cat foods may contain a substance that destroys the B vitamin called thiamine. In the most severe form of thiamine deficiency, these cats can develop depression and seizures.

Some disease conditions can result in a vitamin depletion. Because the water-soluble vitamins are not stored in the body, they will be depleted rapidly if a cat is allowed to go without food for even a few days, especially if the cat is losing a lot of body water from kidney disease, vomiting, or diarrhea. Diseases that result in improper absorption of fats, such as liver diseases, will of course affect the absorption of the fat-soluble vitamins, too. Because fat-soluble vitamins are in reserve, problems related to deficiencies in these vitamins usually occur after a longer period of time.

Vitamin excesses are potentially a problem when cats are being fed home-cooked diets. It is very difficult to balance these diets with the proper nutrient levels, because the batches are small and the vitamin sources are quite concentrated in comparison. Vitamin excesses are also a potential problem for cats that are given vitamin supplements in their diets or as treats. *Never give a vitamin supplement unless you are instructed to do so by your veterinarian.*

A healthy diet shows in a Maine coon's coat, eyes, and disposition.

Minerals serve as important structural components in the body. Calcium, phosphorus, and magnesium make up the matrix of bones and teeth. Sodium and potassium are important in maintaining cell shape and in nerve conduction. Calcium is also needed for muscles to contract. Minerals such as iron and copper are needed for proper red blood cell function. Zinc is important for healthy skin.

Minerals are needed in very trace amounts in the diet. They are provided by both plant and animal sources, however, most of the mineral in cat foods comes from bonemeal and meat meals used in formulating the diets. Poor quality and cheap meat ingredients used in making cat foods have a lot of bone in them. This bone is expensive to remove from the meat scraps, so it is usually just left in with it. Most cat foods contain minerals in amounts that far exceed the requirements for the cat. This is especially true for fish-containing diets. These excessive minerals have to be eliminated from the cat's body, usually in the urine.

Ash refers to the residue that is left when a diet is burned to completion. You can think about ash as being basically the same substance as the residue in your fireplace or in your wood stove. Ash is a mineral residue. The name does not specify which minerals or how much of any one there may be in the mix.

Water is the most important of the six basic nutrients. Most animals cannot live more than a short time without it, or more than a few days without becoming dehydrated and sick. Water comprises about 95 percent of the newborn animal to about 75 percent of the adult. Water is the body's primary solvent for chemical reactions and life processes, and maintains cell shape. Throughout the animal kingdom, animals have evolved elaborate adaptive mechanisms to conserve water. The kidney is of paramount importance in this role. And cats, originally from the African desert, are particularly efficient at conserving water and producing very concentrated urine.

Cats are classified as true carnivores, that is, they are true meat-eating animals because proteins and fats from animal-tissue sources must be consumed. This is because of several major reasons. First, the essential amino acid taurine and the essential fatty acid arachidonic are only present in animal tissues. Secondly, of the vitamins, cats cannot convert beta-carotene from plants into vitamin A, nor can they convert biotin into the B vitamin called niacin. Both of these vitamins must therefore come from animal tissues. Cats, unlike dogs, require some of their energy to come from protein, and have higher requirements for some specific amino acids and vitamins. For all of these reasons, cats should not be fed diets formulated for dogs.

Choosing a Diet for a Healthy Cat

There are three types of cat food from which you can choose: dry kibble, canned, and semimoist formulations. The difference between the three is basically in the amount of moisture contained in each product. Most dry cat foods contain about 10 to 12 percent moisture. Canned foods vary between 78 to 82 percent, and semimoist foods are approximately 25 to 39 percent moisture. Semimoist foods contain various chemical preservatives to keep the food in its spongy, semimoist state. Semimoist foods are also fairly high in sugar.

Because these foods differ primarily in moisture content, there is little nutritional advantage to feeding canned food over dry food. Canned food looks more like meat, and because your Maine coon cat is a carnivore, you may assume in error that the canned food is more appropriate. Canned foods may be better for cats that don't drink enough water on their own. Some cats may also find canned foods are easier to digest. The cans themselves are recyclable and are therefore more environmentally friendly. Canned food tends to stick to the teeth and promote plaque and tartar buildup and periodontal disease. It's doubly important to brush your Maine coon cat's teeth if it's eating canned food.

Dry kibble foods are just as nutritious, less expensive, and more convenient. Dry foods are less likely to promote dental disease. If you choose to feed your pet both, that's fine. I personally avoid semimoist foods because of the addition of chemicals to keep them soft and moist, the higher sugar content, and their greater tendency to be artificially colored. None of these characteristics is particularly beneficial to your Maine coon cat.

It is far more important to pay attention to the quality of the food that you

Kittens have special feeding requirements because their stomachs are so small. Either give your pet free access to dry kibble by leaving a bowl on the floor at all times or offer it small servings of canned food several times a day.

choose, rather than if it comes in a can or a bag. How do you know about the quality? Most owners try to decide this by reading the labels for the ingredients and the guaranteed analysis of crude protein, fat, minerals, and so on; both are heavily influenced by advertising and can be very misleading.

For example: Because the moisture content of cat foods varies from brand to brand and flavor to flavor, you cannot simply compare the guaranteed analysis listed on the label of the nutrient content from one brand to another. The difference in the amount of water means that a dry food A that has 10 percent water will not have the same amount of protein as a dry food B that has 12 percent moisture, even if both labels indicate 22 percent. Dry food B will actually have *less* protein in it than dry food A because of the higher water content.

Why is this important? Because unless you evaluate the nutrients in foods on a dry matter or dehydrated basis, you cannot compare the guaranteed analysis for nutrient content. The guaranteed analysis on a can or bag almost always lists nutrients on an *as fed basis, or with the water left in.* The guaranteed analysis is not a list of the exact amounts of each nutrient either. The words "not less than" or "not more than" indicate that the percentages are indeed approximations.

Likewise, the ingredients list on a label can also be misleading depending upon the order in which they are listed and the wording used to describe the ingredients themselves. One company's "chicken meal" may not be the same quality as another company's. For these reasons, it is very important to rely on the manufacturer's reputation for quality when you choose a food for your Maine coon cat.

Seek the advice of those who know about nutrition: your veterinarian and Maine coon cat breeder. Be a smart consumer and try to recognize and avoid the marketing hype and cute packaging, and choose your Maine coon cat's food based on sound scientific principles. The only indication of quality on a cat food label is the manufacturer's logo. Compile a list of specific questions about a brand of cat food and call the toll-free telephone number listed on the bag or can. The manufacturer's nutritional consultants should be able to provide you with the answers.

Keep in mind that you get what you pay for. A rule of thumb: The higher-priced premium brands are generally made with better quality ingredients. Here are some specific features that you should insist upon:

Fixed formulation: These foods are prepared using the same set of ingredients in every batch. Unless the label says "fixed formulation," you should assume that the manufacturer uses the ingredients that are the least

Cat food comes in three formulations: dry, canned, and semimoist.

expensive at the time. The Food and Drug Administration (FDA) does not require that the label on the can or box be changed for six months. For this reason, what you see on the label may not actually be what is in the product.

Digestibility: Highly digestible diets mean that more nutrients are actually available to the cat. There is less waste to clean out of the litter box. Your Maine coon cat will have to eat less, which means it will cost less to feed a highly digestible food. This is especially important for kittens. Kittens must consume much larger quantities of poorly digestible diets in order to obtain adequate calories and nutrients for growth and development, which may be impossible with their small stomach capacity.

Palatability: The most nutritious diet in the world is useless unless a cat will actually eat it. Fat, protein, salt, temperature, acidity or alkalinity, and texture are very important palatability factors for cats. These can be used to coax a cat to eat when it's not feeling well. Some of these factors, salt for instance, can be very harmful. On the other hand, just because a diet is palatable, that doesn't mean that it is nutritious or even good for your cat. As an example, diets made with beef tallow are very palatable for cats, but it is known that beef tallow is a relatively poor quality source of essential fatty acids. Fish, also extremely palatable, contains potentially harmful excesses of minerals and possibly substances that destroy thiamine or cause pansteatitis.

Balanced for the stage in the cat's life: Nutrient requirements change depending upon the life stage of the cat. The energy and nutrient requirements for a growing kitten and pregnant queen are nearly double that of a nonpregnant adult cat. If a cat food is labeled "for all stages of growth and maintenance," you should be aware that that food is formulated to meet the greater needs of kittens and pregnant adults and could contain excessive amounts of nutrients that may be harmful to the nonpregnant adult cat and cats with certain diseases.

The FDA requires that pet food manufacturers provide a "statement of nutritional purpose" on every label. The statement will indicate to which life stage(s) the food is intended to be fed and should be according to the Association of American Feed Control Officials (AAFCO) guidelines. The FDA no longer allows cat foods to be formulated according to National Research Council (NRC) guidelines. Any cat foods bearing an NRC statement is considered improperly labeled. Do not feed these foods to your Maine coon cat or kitten.

Feeding Recommendations

Maine coon kittens should be fed canned or dry food formulated specifically for kittens. Check the label for the appropriate AAFCO statement to confirm this. As a general rule, kittens should be fed "free choice" until about one year of age. After your Maine coon kitten has been neutered, monitor its body weight and appearance carefully. The body's metabolism slows some after neutering and excessive food intake will result in obesity.

Allow your kitten access to a bowl of dry kibble at all times. Don't overfill the bowl, or add more food on top of kibble that has been sitting out for more than 24 hours, to avoid feeding rancid food. If you choose to feed your Maine coon kitten canned food, feed it separately from the dry, and do not leave canned food out for more than an hour or so. Canned foods are often preservative-free and will spoil, especially in warm weather.

If you choose to feed your kitten canned food exclusively, you will need to feed it small meals several times a day. Remember that about 80 percent of canned foods are water and your kitten's stomach is small, so it must eat frequently in order to obtain adequate nutrients to support normal growth.

Feed nonpregnant adult Maine coon cats a balanced diet formulated for maintenance of nonreproducing adults. The diet should be very digestible and a fixed formulation. The food should also be moderately restricted in magnesium, containing approximately 20 milligrams of magnesium per 100 kcals of the food. And when fed free choice, the food should produce a moderately acidic urine. Overly acidified diets can lead to osteoporosis and kidney disease.

Except under special circumstances when your veterinarian instructs you to do so, do not feed your Maine coon cat a home-cooked diet. These diets are extremely difficult to balance and could result in life-threatening nutritional diseases when fed over a long period of time. Do not feed your Maine coon cat a vegetarian diet. Cats are obligate carnivores; vegetarian diets are unnatural and extremely harmful. Likewise, do not feed your Maine coon cat cooked organ meats such as beef heart or liver, as they are also very deficient in certain nutrients and could lead to severe health problems if a significant calorie intake is from organ meats.

Behaviorists tell us that the average cat eats about 16 times a day. Your Maine coon cat should naturally eat the amount of food necessary to meet its energy needs. However, the texture, salt content, kibble shape, coatings, and so on, influence the palatability of the food and thus your cat's food intake. Because of palatability enhancements, your cat may eat more than its body needs for energy and become obese. Obesity is one of the most common problems afflicting pets. For this reason, you should mon-

Mother cats will take care of feeding their kittens for about the first month of life. They will nurse their newborns within the first hour, then will continue to nurse on demand until the youngsters are about 4 to 5 weeks old.

itor and possibly restrict the food intake of your Maine coon to prevent this from being its problem, too!

Begin with a food that meets the basic formulation requirements and then consider the calorie content. Calorie content is now permitted to be listed on the labels of pet foods and it will be showing up there more frequently. The average, active adult cat requires about 30 kcal per pound (65 kcal per kg) of body weight for maintenance. Overweight cats will require 20 to 30 percent fewer calories. If you know the calorie content of the food you intend to feed, you can calculate your Maine coon cat's approximate calorie needs based on its body weight and condition and adjust the manufacturer's feeding recommendations on the bag or can accordingly. If your adult Maine coon cat tends to be inactive or overweight, choose the "lite" or "less active" formula of the diet.

If you feed your Maine coon cat exclusively dry food, it is perfectly appropriate to fill its bowl with a measured amount of food once a day and allow it to eat at its own times. Use a dry measuring cup to measure the food; do not rely on estimates of the amount. Small inaccuracies in measurement will result in significant differences in calorie intake. If you find that your cat eats too fast because the food is so palatable and your pet's mellifluous yet unceasing cries call you back into the kitchen for more, divide the daily food allotment into two to four portions and dole them out at intervals throughout the day.

If you choose to feed canned food as well, reduce the amount of dry food that you offer for free choice. As with kittens, feed the canned food separately and leave it out for only a short while to prevent spoilage. Exclusively canned food diets will require that you feed your pet several times a day.

What about fat cats? Despite your best efforts, your Maine coon cat may still become fat. If it goes outdoors, it could be supplementing its regular fare with small prey or snacking at a neighbor's. It is known that obesity is an unhealthy condition in other animals, causing stress on the cardiovascular and musculoskeletal systems and shortening life span. Although this has not yet been proven to be so in cats, the tendency is to extrapolate these potential problems to them. It is known for certain that obese cats have a greater risk of at least one form of liver disease and diabetes. Obese cats are greater surgical and anesthetic risks, too.

Weight loss is difficult to achieve in cats. Some obese cats seem to exist on so little food that dietary restriction appears impossible. And exercise, the key component of successful weight reduction, is also elusive. Its just so hard to motivate that fat cat to do anything aerobic. That's why prevention is the key.

Weight loss in overweight cats requires a reduction in their calorie intake by 30 to 40 percent. The reduction should be gradual, but feeding less of the normal diet is not appropriate. The volume of food that you might need to feed to achieve that degree of calorie restriction may be too small to be satisfying to your Maine coon cat's appetite and could lead to nutrient deficiencies.

Note: The "lite" or "less active" formulations of most cat foods are usually not sufficiently restricted in calories to affect weight loss. The best foods for dieting your Maine coon cat are prescription-type diets available from your veterinarian. Weight loss should be attempted only under the supervision of your veterinarian to minimize the chance of your Maine

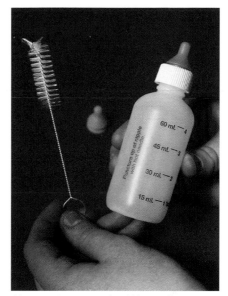

Use a pet nurser to feed kittens that are too weak to nurse or that have been orphaned. Shown above are a standard pet nurser, nipple, and bottle brush, available in pet shops and from veterinarians.

coon cat developing hepatic lipidosis as a result of the calorie restriction.

Healthy, senior Maine coon cats do not require special diets. "Senior" cat foods are making their way onto the supermarket shelves. These are "designer" cat foods created by pet food marketing departments hoping that the pet owner who already recognizes the need for diet changes in their older dog will assume that the same is also true for their older cat and as a result, buy this cat food. Unlike dogs, healthy, older cats have not been demonstrated to have special nutritional requirements. Their ability to digest foods does not diminish with advancing age. You may feed your geriatric Maine coon cat the same way you did when he was a young adult, except if disease should occur.

Older cats that develop certain diseases may require dietary restrictions

73

or enhancement of certain nutrients. Kidney disease and cancer are two examples. Geriatric cats may also have dental disease that necessitates feeding soft foods. (Although tooth loss does not preclude feeding dry kibble, cats swallow most of their kibble whole.) Most dietary management involves the use of prescription-type diets and supplements from your veterinarian. This would be the exception to the "feed your older Maine coon cat the same as you would your younger adult" rule.

Pregnant and nursing Maine coon cats also have special nutritional requirements. They require two or more times the energy of nonreproducing females. The feti also need energy, protein, fats, minerals, and vitamins for growth and development. Once the kittens are born, nursing mothers need more nutrients for milk production and restoration of body condition lost during pregnancy.

The gestational period for cats is in the range of 64 to 69 days. You should switch your Maine coon cat from a high-quality adult maintenance diet to a kitten food during the last trimester of pregnancy, until the kittens are weaned. The last trimester begins around day 45 after breeding and the kittens are weaned at about six weeks of age. Your pregnant or nursing Maine coon cat should be allowed free access to dry kitten kibble. Canned kitten food is again optional, but as the kittens approach weaning, it is helpful to offer the mother canned food so that the kittens can also begin eating solid food.

Mother cat will feed her newborn kittens. Newborns should nurse within the first hour of birth in order to receive the antibody-rich first milk or colostrum that will provide the kittens with immunity to infectious diseases until their own immune systems develop. Mother cat allows her kittens to nurse on demand until about four or five weeks

of age. Then she will not be as accommodating to their demands and begin to avoid them. Kittens learn to eat solid food by observing the mother. You can offer the kittens a slurry of canned kitten food mixed with water or milk replacement (see My tip, below). Gradually eliminate the water and feed kitten food alone.

Weak or orphaned kittens should be bottle-fed every two to four hours with an appropriate milk replacement such as KMR. Do not use the milk substitutes sold at supermarkets. These are not nutritionally complete. Complete and balanced milk replacements are sold at pet stores and through veterinarians. They come in canned or powdered form that you reconstitute with tap water.

My tip: Use the powdered form of milk replacement. That way you can reconstitute only what you need for a 24-hour period. Pre-prepared formulas must be discarded after a short period after opening and this is wasteful and expensive.

At the same time that you purchase milk replacement, also purchase a pet nurser. These are about the same size as a doll's bottle. Before you use the nurser, you must cut a hole in the nipple. One of the biggest mistakes people make when they're trying to bottle-feed kittens is to simply pierce the end of the nipple with a needle. When the kitten tries to nurse, very little milk is released unless you cut a hole large enough for a drop of milk to form when the bottle is inverted.

Warm about 2 ounces (60 mL) of milk replacement to *body temperature* by standing the nurser in a pan of warm water. Offer this to your kitten about every two hours. Unless it's very weak, it'll let you know when it's time to eat! Newborn kittens do not urinate or defecate on their own; the mother must stimulate them to do so by licking the perineum. To keep the nest clean, the mother consumes the urine and feces. After feeding the kitten, stroke the perineum with a piece of absorbent cotton moistened with warm water, to mimic the stimulation provided by the mother.

Very weak kittens will need to be tube-fed the milk replacement. You should contact your veterinarian and bring weak kittens to the hospital for examination. Your veterinarian can show you how to tube-feed the kitten at home if necessary.

Bottle-fed kittens can be transitioned to solid food using a slurry of canned kitten food and milk replacement. Push your Maine coon kitten's little face into the slurry. It should suck on the mixture at first and catch on quickly. Alternatively, put its paw into the mixture and let it lick the paw clean.

Table scraps and nutritional supplements: Complete and balanced diets are made so that every mouthful of food contains just the right amount of each nutrient that your Maine coon cat needs for growth and maintenance. If you add table scraps, supplements, or vitamins to your pet's food, its diet becomes unbalanced and it is likely to consume more calories than it needs. Why reinvent the wheel? If you choose a high-quality diet, scientifically formulated in the first place, you do not need to supplement the diet. It already has been done for you!

Your Maine coon cat should have free access to fresh water at all times. Wash the water bowl with hot, soapy water regularly to prevent bacterial and fungal growth (that's that slimy feeling in the bowl). Do not give milk to your Maine coon cat or kitten. Cats cannot digest the sugar called lactose in milk, but the bacteria that colonize their intestinal tract can. This bacterial digestion of the milk sugar can cause diarrhea or loose stools.

Cat with different nutritional needs: An example of this might be a

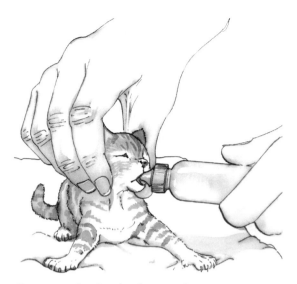

Be very gentle when feeding a newborn or weak kitten with a bottle. Carefully hold the kitten's head steady with one hand while holding the bottle in a horizontal (not vertical) position with the other hand. The kitten will nurse until it is satisfied.

household that has one fat cat and one cat that is at a good body weight. This is a difficult question because the answer usually means having to change long-standing feeding patterns. In this specific example, I usually suggest that a measured amount of calorie-restricted kibble be fed to both cats free choice or in intermittent allotments during the day. The cat with the normal body weight could also be given a portion of canned maintenance diet separately, so that its calorie needs are met. Although cats normally eat several times a day, they can adjust to being meal-fed, as dogs are fed. Your Maine coon cat may be rather vocal about this adjustment, but you must weigh the benefits of changing its accustomed feeding schedule with the sassing it is giving you.

Here are some other suggestions. Always try to strive for the ideal situation in the long term, but if you cannot, do the best that you can:

1. Feed the restricted diet to all; supplement the ones that do not need restriction with extra meals. For example: Kittens can be allowed to nibble on adult maintenance but should be fed canned kitten food separately two or three times a day to insure adequate nutrient intake. Canned food is usually very palatable and it should be no problem getting cats that need supplemental meals to eat.

2. Meal-feed all the cats rather than leave food available at all times. Don't ever be late for supper!

3. Feed in separate locations, closing the cats into separate rooms.

4. Feed them all the same thing. This is appropriate for short periods of time only. For example: Kitten food can be fed to adult cats.

Variety in the diet: Your Maine coon cat needs six basic nutrients: proteins, carbohydrates, fats, vitamins, minerals, and water in order to grow and stay healthy. Cat foods made with high-quality ingredients and formulated to meet AAFCO standards by well-known manufacturers contain all these nutrients in every single mouthful. All you need to do is add love and a bowl of water. Because these foods are complete, variety is not essential to good nutrition, although some manufacturers spend a lot of money on advertising to convince you otherwise. Frequent diet changes can lead to gastrointestinal upset and diarrhea.

Reproduction and Pregnancy

Initial Considerations

Should you breed *this* cat or should you breed Maine coon cats at all? The considerations for both questions are the same.

Maine coon owners fall in love with the breed and choose to have one because of their historical importance, personality, appearance, and fondness for human companionship. Many bring a kitten home, watch it grow, enjoy its antics and admire its winsome disposition and ability to innocently maneuver the dog and everyone else in the household to do its bidding, then suddenly get the idea to breed more just like this cat… or think: What's going to happen when this cat's gone?

Hold on a minute. Breeding cats, even bringing one litter into this world requires careful pre-thought and consideration of the consequences. A casual breeding, and by that I mean simply having one litter in order to obtain offspring from a favored cat, or to give the kids the opportunity to witness the "miracle of birth," is a serious undertaking. There are significant costs and expenses and risks. There is a very high probability of contributing to the unwanted pet population. Even if you pre-place the offspring into homes, you no longer have any control over those kittens. Chance breedings may occur that contribute to the cycle of birth–abandonment–suffering–death. Purebred cats and dogs are not exempt from this despair.

Consider also, the risks to the queen. Pregnancy and delivery put major physiologic demands on the body; they are draining on the mother. If surgical intervention is necessary, the mother and/or the kittens may die. If your initial intention was to have an offspring of your cherished Maine coon, how would you feel if you lost her in the process?

After paying the purchase price for a purebred cat, some people get the notion that there is money to be made in breeding. After all, if the breeder sold four Maine coon kittens for $550 apiece, why that's more than $2,000!

As kittens mature, their curiosity carries them further and further from the nest.

Before you run out and put a down payment on that sailboat you've been wanting in anticipation of big profits, be aware that the serious Maine coon breeder has a considerable investment of time, energy, and money into a pursuit that is largely a hobby. Here are some of the costs:

1. Purchasing a breeding queen. The price will be higher, upward of $800, for a show-quality kitten from champion lines. There are plenty of long-haired, fluffy pet cats in this world. Unless the cat is of show quality, there's no reason to breed it.

2. Stud fees. This includes an initial cash payment to allow a female to breed with a male. Some stud owners also ask for first choice of a kitten from the litter as part of the payment. Stud fees include transporting the queen to the stud for breeding.

3. Purchasing a stud. In lieu of breeding to an outside source, some breeders keep a male cat. Naturally the male should be from champion lines also. There's another $800 or more.

4. Health maintenance medical care. Routine examinations, vaccinations, feline leukemia virus, feline immunodeficiency virus, or other serologic tests, fecal examinations for parasites, and parasiticides including flea-control products are the minimal expenses involved. Multiply this cost times the number of Maine coon cats kept for breeding.

5. Veterinary care for the kittens. Reputable breeders will pay for the initial examinations, vaccinations, and parasite control prior to sale or adoption.

6. Nonroutine medical care. Fertility and infertility workups, problems during pregnancy or delivery such as cesarean sections, care for weak, unthrifty kittens, and illnesses not related to breeding are unknown variables. This cost will also vary depending upon the number of cats in the cattery.

7. Supplies. This includes cages, litter boxes, fillers, scoops, liners, food and water bowls, beds, grooming needs, carriers, toys, and equipment needed for cat shows.

8. Food. This is one expense that should never be compromised.

9. Association dues, registration fees, entrance fees for shows, travel costs, and other related expenses. Serious breeders campaign their cats.

10. Space within the home. Serious breeders have a "cat room(s)."

11. Time to care for the cats, do the cat room housekeeping, manage the breedings, and promote the cats. This can be a full-time job.

If you dearly love your Maine coon cat and wish to have another, go back to the breeder where you purchased it. Leave the breeding to the experts unless you have the time and funds to devote to educating yourself about the breed and the responsibilities of breeding. Pet ownership is a privilege, not a right. Pet owners have responsibilities as caretakers of the animals. If you are serious about breeding Maine coon cats and understand that you need to contribute back to the breed, get involved in the MCBFA (see Associations, page 108). Visit with as many established breeders as you can. Plan carefully.

Sexing Cats

When kittens are first born, the external genitalia may be precociously developed making it easy to distinguish the males from the females. Within a day or so, the genitalia is no longer so unique and it becomes difficult to identify the male kittens from female kittens again until they are a couple of weeks old. Male kittens will have a round opening to the prepuce that is positioned directly under the anus. As the male kitten matures into adolescence, the genitalia become more distinct. The testicles enlarge in the scrotal sac and appear as two bulges side-by-side, in the space below the anus and just above the prepucial opening. As a tom cat matures sexually, he will develop barbs or spines on his penis. Intact (unneutered) male cats have larger heads and prominent jowls than neutered males.

Females have a slitlike opening under the anus, which is the vulva. The vulva will elongate slightly as the female matures. Female cats do not develop jowls.

Courtship and Mating

Both male and female Maine coon cats begin to develop sexually around five to nine months of age. In females, called queens, this is when estrus, also called heat cycles begin to occur. Estrous cycles have two parts: a characteristic set of behaviors that attract male cats and encourage mating, and secondly, a series of physiologic events that include ovulation, conception, gestation, birth, and recovery. Female dogs in heat can be recognized by a swelling of the vulva and bloody vaginal discharge. This is not true for cats. Other than by her behavior, a female cat shows no obvious external signs of estrus.

Early estrous behaviors begin with your female Maine coon showing increasing affection toward you or inanimate objects by rubbing her head or body on people or things. She may stretch provocatively and roll on the ground. Cats in heat will vocalize more, emitting long, whining, sometimes unnatural sounds. Although it may sound contradictory, some females become unpredictably aggressive and suddenly strike out when

Gender is easy to determine in a cat. The little Maine coon on the left is a male, and the kitten on the right is a female.

approached by a male cat or person. As the female becomes more receptive to breeding, she will tread on her back feet if stroked above her tail. When treading, the hindquarters are held high and the chest and abdomen are pressed close to the ground while stepping her rear feet up and down.

Along with these behaviors, chemical markers in vaginal secretions, in urine, and from the scent glands located in the relatively hairless areas below the ears, attract male cats called toms. Recognizing that the female is receptive by the treading behavior, the tom will mount her and grasp the skin on her neck in his teeth. Intromission and ejaculation occur quickly. As the tom begins to retreat, the female screams and turns on him aggressively. The female then rolls on the ground and licks her vulva. Copulation is repeated several times over a few hours.

If your sexually receptive Maine coon cat successfully encounters a male, her estrous behaviors disappear in about 24 hours. If breeding does not occur, the behaviors wane after

The mothering of kittens is best left to the mother cat. Here, a Maine coon mom washes her little one.

several days, then cease altogether for a variable number of days. Estrous behaviors then reappear and she will continue to cycle in and out of estrus for several weeks.

Female Maine coon cats are capable of going into heat anytime throughout the year, however, most females will not exhibit estrus in the late fall through midwinter. Peak cycling times occur again in the late winter and in the early summer. Keep in mind that estrous behavior is not always that dramatic or obvious in young cats and you may not recognize it. Your adolescent Maine coon cat can become pregnant during her first estrous cycle. She should be isolated from any males until she is spayed or the breeding can be planned.

Male cats do not have heat cycles; they are receptive to females and eager to breed any time of the year. Sexual maturity in males is exhibited by their territorial behaviors, i.e., urine spraying and aggression toward other rival males. Sexual maturity is displayed physically by the more substantial body size and condition including the head and jowls that develop under the influence of the hormone testosterone.

Gestation and Delivery

Sexual intercourse induces the ovaries to release eggs. The eggs are fertilized and then implant into the wall of the uterus where they develop into embryos, then feti, then kittens. The normal gestation time for cats is 64 to 69 days. Within 48 hours of delivery, the pregnant queen's body temperature will drop below normal to about 100°F (37.8°C) and she will begin to look for a place to have the kittens. If you are unsure of the delivery date, you can check your Maine coon cat's temperature for this predictable drop. Secluded nesting places are preferred, but the social nature of the Maine coon cat may allow her to deliver her kittens in the company of her owner. The mother should be isolated from all other cats.

Labor and delivery proceed quietly. Your cat will act restless and shift her position frequently at first, and lick her vulva often. As the birth approaches, she will lie on her side and her respirations will be quick and shallow. Strong contractions will undulate across her abdomen and she will strain to deliver a kitten with the contraction. The kitten is born enclosed within or partially within a set of membranes. The mother opens the membranes with her teeth if they have not been torn during passage through the birth canal. She then licks the kitten to stimulate its respirations and to clean the birth fluids from its nose and mouth.

As the mother continues to lick and clean the membranes and fluids from the kitten, she will encounter the umbilical cord at the kitten's abdomen, attached to the placenta, which is usually delivered after the kitten. The mother separates the kitten from the placenta by chewing the cord close to the body, and nudges it toward her mammary glands to nurse. The placenta is a pulpy mass of blood vessels that surrounded the kitten's abdomen while it was in the uterus. The placenta provides nourishment from the mother during development. After delivery of the placenta, the mother eats it and the membrane remnants unless someone is there to remove it.

The normal number of kittens in a litter of Maine coons is from three to five although some breeders report up to eight. The remaining kittens in a litter are born in reasonably close succession, about 30 minutes between deliveries, over a few hours. Your Maine coon mother may stop the delivery if she is disturbed, and she may move the nest mid-delivery. Extended pauses of up to 24 hours may occur if the litter was conceived from matings with more than one male. Again, these pauses are normal. You should be concerned if your Maine coon cat is actively but unsuccessfully straining to deliver a kitten for 45 minutes or more.

Do not interfere with the delivery.

After delivery, your new mother will spend most of her time nursing and cleaning her newborns. She herself may not eat very much at first; if she's been allowed to eat the placentas, she won't be hungry. Continue to feed her a high-quality diet formulated for kittens and pregnant queens for the next five or six weeks until the kittens are weaned in order to provide her with adequate energy and nutrients for recovery of her body condition and milk production. Her requirement for water will also be increased because of the demands for milk production. Have fresh water available for her all the time. (See Feeding Recommendations, page 71.)

Problems with Pregnancy and Delivery

Problems with pregnancy are fewer in cats than in other species of animals, and include infertility; failure to carry the pregnancy to term, resulting in resorption of the feti, abortions, and stillbirths; birth of deformed kittens (live or dead) due to genetics or prenatal factors; and uterine infections. Common causes of problems related to pregnancy include inadequate attention to prenatal care such as the environmental stress of weather extremes in cats allowed outdoors, large numbers of cats or other animals kept together, aggression between animals; poor nutrition; and failure to vaccinate properly and exposure to infectious agents such as feline leukemia virus. Stillbirths are reportedly seen more often in Maine coon cats, and this is probably genetically related. To eliminate this genetic predisposition from the breed, a Maine coon cat that repeatedly gives birth to litters with dead kittens, and her offspring, should not be used for further breeding.

A problem delivery is termed dystocia and usually refers to a failure to deliver kittens in a coordinated and timely manner because of either fetal or maternal factors. These factors range from a kitten being too large to pass through the birth canal or weakness on the part of the mother. Any pre-existing problems with the pregnancy can cause dystocia, but primary dystocia can occur unexpectedly even with an uneventful pregnancy. In my experience, problems with pregnancy are more common than primary dystocia. Any of the following signs may indicate problems with either the pregnancy or the delivery:

1. Vaginal discharge other than at the time of delivery. Normal birthing discharge should be reddish blood. Any bluish bloody discharge, pus, or foul odor is abnormal.

2. Failure to deliver a kitten after active straining for 45 minutes.
3. Failure of a kitten to progress through the birth canal.
4. Kittens born deformed, weak, or dead.
5. Death of kittens soon after birth.
6. Rejection of kitten(s) by the mother.
7. Gestation time greater than 69 days.
8. Failure of the kittens to grow and develop normally.

The appearance of any of these signs should prompt you to call your veterinarian. The mother and the kittens, including any that have died, should be examined.

Newborn Care

Nursing during the first few hours of life is critical to newborn kittens. This is when they ingest colostrum, or the first milk produced by the mother's mammary glands. Colostrum is rich in antibodies that will be absorbed by the kittens and provide immunity to infectious diseases. The immune system of kittens and other newborn animals is undeveloped at birth. They are susceptible to all infectious disease unless protected by these maternally derived antibodies. This type of immunity is termed passive immunity as opposed to the active immunity of one's own immune system.

Newborn kittens have the ability to absorb these antibodies for only a few hours after birth. Colostrum given after that window of opportunity for absorption will not impart any passive immunity. Likewise, colostrum from mothers who have not been properly vaccinated against infectious diseases will not contain adequate amounts of protective antibodies. Newborn kittens nursing from such a mother will not be protected. Sometimes, even if a mother received timely prenatal vaccinations, a kitten doesn't absorb antibodies from the colostrum. This may be due to some physiologic factors and explains why some newborn kittens fail to thrive.

Newborn kittens spend most of their time sleeping during the first 14 to 17 days, waking briefly to nurse. They nurse preferentially from one teat. Movements during nursing and sleeping are important to the development of their motor skills as they grow. Your Maine coon mother won't leave them except to eat or use the litter box. Because newborns do not urinate or defecate by reflex, she must stimulate them to do so by licking the perineum, and she consumes the feces and urine to keep the nest clean.

Newborn kittens don't maintain their body temperature on their own, and stay warm through contact with the mother. The mother may push a weak or sick kitten out of the nest. Rarely will a mother abandon an apparently normal kitten or the entire litter. When kittens are removed or pushed from the nest, they become cold very quickly. Once the body temperature drops below 96°F (35.6°C), a kitten can't absorb nutrients from milk and so normal body functions like respiration and circulation fail. Such a kitten can die within a few hours.

Just as you should not intervene in the delivery of kittens, you should not interfere with the mothering either. Your primary role should be to make sure that the kittens are nursing and stay within the nest. If you see that one or more of your kittens is straying from the mother, crying excessively or failing to nurse, put it back next to the mother and consider using a supplemental heating source such as a lightbulb, heating pad, or hot water bottle. If the problem persists, contact your veterinarian.

At about 17 days of age, the kittens' ears and then eyes will open and they will begin to explore the nest in a bobbing, uncoordinated, and very vocal fashion. At three weeks of age, the kittens are more coordinated and they begin to exhibit play-behavior that is important in developing the skills necessary for recognizing, stalking, and hunting prey.

As the kittens become more active and independent, your Maine coon mother will spend more time away from them. She will not be available to nurse on demand and eventually she will completely refuse to do so. Begin to make available a high-quality, very digestible, canned kitten food at about four or five weeks of age to facilitate this weaning. The kittens should be handled gently and frequently beginning about this age, to socialize them to humans. Exposure to other pets such as dogs, birds, and rats during this time will socialize these kittens to other animals too. This will make the kittens more affable toward other pets in their new homes. Of course, who could resist anyway! It is important that the kittens remain with their mother and siblings until they are at least eight or nine weeks old.

It is vital that newborns nurse within the first few hours of life. This is when their bodies are able to absorb the antibodies from their mother's colostrum that provide immunity to infectious diseases.

To protect the young kittens from infectious diseases, do not allow them contact with other older kittens and cats. If you have other cats, feed and care for the kittens first before you handle the older ones. Kittens can go to new homes as early as eight weeks of age, but ten weeks is better.

In Sickness and in Health

Preventative Health Care

Vaccinations

Along with regular checkups, proper nutrition, and dental care, vaccinations are an important part of keeping your Maine coon cat healthy (see Recommended Vaccinations chart, following). Many infectious diseases of cats can be prevented or at least reduced in severity by timely and proper vaccination. Even if your Maine coon cat has no direct exposure to other cats found outdoors, in a boarding facility or cattery, or through cat shows, your pet should be vaccinated against feline viral rhinotracheitis, calicivirus, chlamydia, and panleukopenia, which are highly contagious, and rabies, which is always fatal and probably required by law in your area.

Newborn kittens receive passive immunity from their mothers when they nurse for the first time. Antibodies in colostrum provide protection against infectious diseases until the kitten's immune system can take over. Maternally-derived antibodies don't last forever; passive antibody levels wane over several weeks.

Your Maine coon kitten's own active immune system is ready for challenge when it is about eight weeks old. Passively acquired antibodies that still circulate in its body will interfere with any vaccination that it is given, so it will not develop a very strong response to the initial vaccine.

Because there is no practical way to know exactly when the maternal antibody is gone, kittens should be given booster vaccinations at three- to four-week intervals until they are 12 to 16 weeks old.

After 16 weeks of age, it is reasonably certain that the mother's antibodies will not be a problem and adolescent and adult cats never before vaccinated are fully capable of responding to a vaccine the first time it is given. These cats (or in the case of a stray with an unknown vaccination status) should be vaccinated twice, three to four weeks apart, against most of the common cat diseases. The first inoculation that is given stimulates the immune system to produce antibodies. The second inoculation "reminds" the immune system and imparts a stronger and more long-lasting response.

Important note: Although Maine coon cats older than 16 weeks of age probably do not have enough maternal antibodies to interfere with the first vaccination, one inoculation is not sufficient to protect them from challenge by an infectious disease. The first time they are given a vaccine, they must be given a series of two inoculations to have long-lasting protection.

Yearly boosters with a single dose of vaccine should be given to all adult Maine coon cats in order to keep antibody levels high and the immune response on ready alert. Most of the germs that cause infectious disease in cats are ubiquitous in the environ-

Recommended Vaccinations

Vaccine	Initial	Maintenance
Panleukopenia (FPV)	2 or 3 doses, 4 weeks apart beginning at 8 weeks of age.	Yearly. Special vaccine required for pregnant queens.
Calicivirus (FCV)	Same as panleukopenia.	Yearly.
Rhinotracheitis (FVR)	Same as panleukopenia.	Yearly.
Chlamydia	Same as panleukopenia.	Yearly.
Feline Infectious Peritonitis (FIP)	2 doses 4 weeks apart beginning at 16 weeks of age, in high-risk catteries, households, and shelters where virus is endemic.	Yearly.
Feline Leukemia Virus (FeLV)	2 or 3 doses, 4 weeks apart only after a negative FeLV test.	Yearly.
Rabies	Dose at 3 months of age, then 1 year later.	According to local laws or manufacturer's recommendation. Precautionary after: 1. every wound of unknown origin; 2. every bite wound from animal with unknown vaccination history; 3. every bite from animal with lapsed vaccinations.

ment, and cats come in contact with them more often than you may be aware. Contact with other cats outdoors and in boarding situations are obvious modes of exposure. Some viruses are extremely hardy and can survive long enough outside of the body to be transmitted by you to your Maine coon cat on your hands and clothing if you come in contact with other cats. Yearly vaccination is a wise insurance policy.

Your geriatric Maine coon cat: You may be tempted to think that after several years of vaccination, surely your old Maine coon's immune system has been reminded about those diseases quite enough, thank you, and further vaccination is unnecessary. On the contrary. As your cat ages, so does its immune system and the immune response can wane, leaving your older cat vulnerable to infectious disease once again. Yearly vaccinations are an important part of geriatric care.

Serologic Testing

Serologic testing is a broad category of tests done on serum or blood to determine whether or not an animal is infected or has ever been infected with a specific disease-causing agent such as a virus. The most important serologic test for you and your Maine coon cat is one for feline leukemia virus (FeLV). Regardless of where you purchase your Maine coon kitten, you should make sure that it is serologically negative for this virus. Reputable breeders test their cats for this virus and require proof of a negative test for any cats brought into their cattery. If

Vaccinations should be an integral part of your Maine coon's health-care regime. The proper shots can prevent some infectious diseases and reduce the severity of others.

all of the cats in a cattery or at a private breeder where you purchase your Maine coon have been tested and confirmed to be feline leukemia virus-free, chances are that all the kittens from that source will be as well, and you do not need to test your kitten prior to vaccination.

If the kitten is purchased at a pet store or adopted from a shelter, the feline leukemia virus status at the point of origin for that kitten may not be known. You should request documentation to show that the kitten has been tested negative. If no test has been performed, have the kitten tested at your veterinary hospital as soon as possible, with the sale or adoption agreement contingent upon a negative test.

Important note: Any kitten testing positive for feline leukemia virus should be returned to the breeder, pet store, or shelter. These recommendations also apply to the purchase or adoption of adult Maine coon cats. A single positive test for feline leukemia virus does not necessarily mean that the kitten or cat will remain infected, but you should probably not assume responsibility for that animal. (See Major Infectious Diseases of Cats, page 90.)

My tip: Vaccines are available to protect your Maine coon cat against feline leukemia virus infection. None of the vaccines currently offered afford 100 percent protection against the virus or the diseases that it causes in laboratory trials. However, improvements have been made in these vaccines since they were first introduced, and their safety and efficacy in natural exposure situations warrants their use. If your Maine coon cat is going to go outdoors or will be boarded, have it vaccinated against feline leukemia virus.

Intestinal Parasite Control

Intestinal parasites should not be a problem in kittens and cats acquired through a reputable breeder who prac-

tices conscientious parasite control and keeps the cats indoors. Most intestinal parasites have a fecal-oral route of infection, i.e., the cat becomes infected by ingesting parasite eggs passed in the feces of other cats. Intestinal parasites are a problem when Maine coon cats are allowed outdoors and use toileting areas frequented by other cats. A few parasites are transmitted directly from the mother to her kittens before or shortly after birth. Others are contracted by hunting and eating prey.

In other words, when your Maine coon cat is out hunting in the yard, it may catch more than a rodent. Because many parasites have a life cycle that includes both tissue forms and intestinal forms, infection can go unnoticed and be missed. Once a cat is infected with some parasites, some of the tissue forms can persist in the body despite treatment to eliminate the intestinal ones. These tissue organisms are passed from dam to offspring.

In a well-managed cattery, queens should not be transmitting parasites to the kittens. Intestinal parasites are more likely to be a problem in kittens acquired through casual breeders, pet stores, and shelters. You should have your new Maine coon kitten's feces examined for intestinal parasites at ten or 12 weeks of age. A small amount of fresh stool (about a thimbleful) is all that is necessary. If parasites are found, the appropriate medication will be prescribed and a second fecal examination several weeks after treatment should be done to make sure that the parasites have been eliminated. Some veterinarians (and breeders) advocate routine deworming with safe, effective medications that eliminate the most common intestinal parasites, even if stool analysis does not detect an infection. Throughout adulthood, if your Maine coon cat goes outside, it should have its feces examined once a year at the time of vaccination, especially if it is a hunter. Again, if feces are not available for analysis, deworming with safe prescription medications effective against tapeworms and roundworms should be considered.

My tip: Intestinal parasites are a common cause of vomiting and diarrhea. Always bring a fresh sample of your Maine coon cat or kitten's feces for analysis to your veterinarian at the time of consultation for these problems.

Important note: Some parasitic diseases of cats are transmissible to humans; *Toxoplasma* and roundworms are two examples. Animal parasites, including those that your Maine coon cat may be harboring can cause serious and devastating disease if humans are infected. To prevent human infection, if your cat is at risk for acquiring parasites, have your pet tested regularly and treated appropriately. Dispose of feces safely in such a way that humans are not going to come in contact with it and always wear gloves when gardening in areas where cats eliminate.

Neutering

Unless your Maine coon cat has a temperament and physical characteristics worth preserving and passing on, your pet should be surgically sterilized. Both you and your cat have little to lose by neutering. The claim that neutered cats become obese is untrue unless the cat is also overfed. The mothering experience will not make your female Maine coon cat any more affectionate and will with high probability, contribute to the existing unwanted cat population. Nor will you create sexual frustration.

What you will accomplish by neutering is to eliminate many diseases of the reproductive tract, such as cancers of the testes and infection of the uterus. Objectionable behaviors, such as urine spraying, roaming, and fighting, can be prevented or significantly diminished. The incessant estrous behaviors of the female will also be eliminated. The only disadvantage to neutering is that the sterilization is permanent. Neutered cats can still be exhibited in cat shows in the Premier or Household Pet Class.

If you are uncertain of whether your Maine coon cat is of high show potential, have the breeder from whom you purchased your cat evaluate this potential for you. Your sales agreement may have included a clause giving the breeder the right to use your Maine coon cat for breeding, too. Likewise, you may be obligated by your sales or adoption agreement to neuter your Maine coon cat. If your breeder agrees that your cat should be bred, give that responsibility to your breeder. Leave the breeding to the experts unless you are willing to become an expert yourself.

Neutering your male Maine coon cat involves a surgical procedure called castration, where the testicles are completely removed through an incision in the scrotum. Castration can be performed as early as 12 weeks of age, but most castrations are performed between six and eight months. Some owners inquire about vasectomy as an alternative to castration. Vasectomy involves severing the spermatic ducts leading from the testicles to the penis, leaving the testicles in the scrotum to produce the sex hormone testosterone. There are absolutely no advantages to vasectomy; these males will mark territory with urine and will fight, roam, and pursue females the same as an intact male.

Neutering your female Maine coon cat is usually done at six months of age but again can be done as early as 12 weeks. In surgical sterilization of female cats, both the ovaries and the uterus are removed. This eliminates the hormones responsible for estrous behaviors.

HOW-TO:
Is Your Maine Coon Cat Sick?

Illness is not always an easy thing to detect in cats. Diseases with a mild onset and slow progression are the hardest to recognize because they may minimally disrupt a cat's habits or functioning and the cat slowly adapts. Many owners simply recognize that something is amiss in their cat's behavior, although the exact nature of the problem is obscure. Veterinarians have a term for this: "ADR" for "Ain't Doing Right." Sometimes the answer to why a cat is sick is difficult to see. Cats do tell you what's wrong; they just don't tell you in English.

Organic disease often causes changes in behavior. This can include a decrease or increase in appetite or activity, and seek-

This Maine coon is in physical distress, indicating that something "ain't right."

Frequent trips to the water bowl can be a sign of illness, as can a lack of thirst.

ing secluded places. Even if your cat spends 18 hours a day sleeping, it probably sleeps in several locations during that time. If you come home from work and find it in the same spot it was in when you left in the morning, your pet may not be feeling very well. Failure to use the litter box in an otherwise perfectly trained cat may signal urinary tract or bowel problems. Frequent trips to the water bowl suggests illness, as does lack of drinking.

Frequent coughing and sneezing, labored breathing, repeated vomiting and/or diarrhea, a tilted head, decreased alertness, unnatural aggression, weight gain or loss, voice change, blood in urine, straining to urinate or repeated trips to

the litter box, and limping or crying when handled, are all obvious signs of disease. Many of those signs as well as the more subtle ones can be attributed to lists of problems involving more than one system of the body. Your cat may appear normal on physical examination and still have a serious illness. Depending upon the physical examination findings, additional diagnostic testing including laboratory analysis of blood and urine, radiographs (X rays), ultrasound examinations, biopsies, surgery, and therapeutic trials may be necessary to determine a cause and treatment when a cat is "ADR." You should seek veterinary medical advice early in the course of a suspected illness. Annual physical examination is still your best ally in early detection of disease and disease prevention.

Annual checkups have always been and will always be the best prevenative.

Dental Care

If your Maine coon cat lived wild or feral as its ancestors once did, its diet would consist of whole small animals, skeleton and all. Through the grinding and crunching action of the teeth on bones, its teeth would stay tartar-free for its entire life. Of course your Maine coon would probably die at a fairly young age too, from infectious diseases or accidents and so wouldn't live long enough to develop the severe dental problems seen in domesticated cats that commonly live to between 15 and 20 years.

Routine care at home is the first step toward a lifetime of healthy teeth and gums for your Maine coon cat. Your veterinarian has sponge-tipped swabs and small cat-sized toothbrushes for you to use to brush your Maine coon cat's teeth. Alternatively you can use a cotton swab or a very small child's toothbrush. A veterinary enzymatic toothpaste or oral antiseptic is used to help clean the teeth rather than human toothpaste or mouthwash. Veterinary toothpastes are made in flavors pleasing to your Maine coon cat. Human products are irritating and require that your Maine coon cat rinse its mouth after brushing, which is amusing to think about but ridiculously difficult to get your cat to do.

My tip: Begin brushing your Maine coon cat's teeth with the water from a water-packed cat of tuna fish. After mastering the technique, you can switch to a veterinary enzymatic toothpaste or antiseptic.

Because your Maine coon cat will be amazingly astute about what's about to take place, especially after you've done this once or twice, have the moisten swab or brush ready before you go and engage your pet in this undertaking. Place the cat on a waist-high surface with its back end toward you. With its head held in your hand as you would to give a pill, slide the swab into the back corner of its mouth and gently rub the teeth and gums along the back, sides, and front of your cat's mouth. You don't need to open its mouth to brush the inside or grinding surfaces of the teeth.

From start to finish, it should take about 30 seconds to brush your Maine coon cat's teeth. If you can do this every day, well that's just splendid. If not, try for three times per week. In between brushings or if you absolutely cannot brush your cat's teeth, offer your cat cooked chicken necks to eat once or twice a week. By consuming cooked chicken necks, your Maine coon will be mimicking the natural teeth cleaning process when consuming whole prey.

Regular dental checkups are important to assess how well you're doing with the brushing. Your veterinarian should evaluate your Maine coon cat's teeth at the time of its annual physical examination. Many cats need to have their teeth cleaned and polished with an ultrasonic or rotary scaler like the ones your dentist would use on you. The teeth will be cleaned and examined for cavities, fractures, and loosening. Afterward, they are polished to remove the surface etching. In some cases, a fluoride treatment is used to protect the teeth against cavities. Extractions are also done at this time. Proper dentistry requires general anesthesia.

Some groomers and veterinarians will scrape the teeth as a temporary measure until proper dentistry can be performed. Scraping the teeth by using a hand scaler while the cat is awake chips off the large pieces of tartar, which improves the appearance of the teeth cosmetically and makes it easier for some animals to eat. Because there is no polishing, the etching of the enamel surface of the teeth left by the scaler causes the tartar to rapidly re-form. Because your

Maine coon cat's mouth cannot be thoroughly examined while your pet is awake, cavities and loose teeth cannot be treated.

Important note: Do not substitute the cosmetic removal of tartar for proper dental prophylaxis for your Maine coon cat. Dental disease causes unnecessary pain and can complicate other problems, such as kidney disease, and can certainly shorten your pet's life.

Major Infectious Diseases of Cats

Most of the major infectious diseases of cats can be prevented through timely vaccinations, but vaccines do not provide protection 100 percent of the time. Stress such as that involved in boarding, shipping, poor nutrition, aging, and underlying disease can cause immunosuppression and leave the window of opportunity open for infectious diseases. Improper handling of vaccines, such as that which may occur with over-the-counter biologics, improper vaccination administration, failure to complete a series or receive a booster, will leave a kitten susceptible, too. Exposure to highly virulent strains of a virus or bacteria can overwhelm the immune system even in the face of proper vaccination.

Feline panleukopenia (feline distemper) is a highly contagious disease of cats resembling parvovirus infections in dogs. The infectious agent, a virus, is transmitted between cats through shedding of the virus in the stool of infected cats. Once inside the body, the virus infects the rapidly dividing cells of the lining of the gastrointestinal tract, bone marrow, and lymph nodes. In pregnant cats, the virus invades the developing brain of the kittens.

Cats infected with the panleukopenia virus typically have high fever, vomiting, and diarrhea, and are weak and depressed. The disease is most severe in kittens and unvaccinated adult cats, although some cats harbor the virus in their gastrointestinal tract and do not show illness. Kittens born to mothers infected with the virus late in pregnancy have tremors and difficulty moving and exhibit a typical bunny-hop gait. Treatment for sick cats involves antibiotics to control the secondary bacterial infections, intravenous fluids, and medication to control vomiting. The disease is highly fatal in young kittens.

The virus is very resistant to disinfectants and can survive for long periods of time in the environment once it leaves the body. Asymptomatic carriers—healthy cats shedding the virus from their gastrointestinal tract—contaminate common litter boxes and elimination areas. Susceptible cats and kittens come in contact with the virus, ingest it, and become infected. Serious and fatal cases of feline panleukopenia are preventable by vaccination.

Feline viral rhinotracheitis (FVR) is an upper respiratory viral disease of cats and kittens. Infected cats sneeze frequently and have noisy breathing and a watery to thick mucus or purulent discharge from the nose. Because these cats can't smell their food, they won't eat or drink and become dehydrated. A secondary conjunctivitis is common, with an accumulation of pus and crusty debris around the eyes. In severe cases, ulcers of the cornea and pneumonia occur. As in all infectious diseases, the disease is much worse in kittens that do not have a well-developed immune system.

Supportive care includes force-feeding and fluids and antibiotics given orally and in the eyes to affected kittens and cats. Rhinotracheitis can contribute to the death of seriously ill kittens but is usually not fatal by itself. It can be prevented by proper vaccination. Once infected with this virus, cats become carriers, harboring the virus in their respiratory system, spreading the virus to other cats. Carriers may have periodic and recurrent bouts of the disease when under stress, such as during boarding.

Calicivirus infection is a respiratory disease caused by a virus that is found in almost all cats and kittens. It causes signs similar to those seen in rhinotracheitis infection: sneezing, nasal discharge, and conjunctivitis as well as extensive and painful ulcers in the mouth on the palate and tongue. As expected, these cats won't eat. Fever and pneumonia may develop.

As with any viral infection, treatment involves supportive care in the form of fluids and antibiotics. Appetite stimulants may be given to encourage sick cats to eat. Calicivirus is also not fatal, except in very young kittens that are anorectic for several days and become severely dehydrated.

Vaccination is highly effective in controlling the disease. Once infected with calicivirus, most cats are chronic carriers of the virus and can pass it on to other cats and kittens and can have an occasional mild recrudescence of the disease.

Chlamydial conjunctivitis is an infection of the tissues surrounding the eye in kittens and cats and is caused by a primitive bacteria. The bacteria is readily transmitted from cat to cat through the eye discharge associated with infection. Cats with chlamydial conjunctivitis have recurrent bouts of excessive blinking, tearing, and redness of the tissues around the eyes. The discharge may be thin and watery or thick and cloudy. Topical ointments and oral antibiotics are used for treatment, but chlamydial conjunctivitis is difficult or impossible to cure. A vaccination is available to help control this recurrent disease.

Feline leukemia virus (FeLV) causes several different diseases in cats and has been implicated as a complicating factor in many cat illnesses. The leukemia virus causes two different classes of disease: cancerous and noncancerous.

Important note: The name feline leukemia virus is very misleading. The virus does indeed cause cancer of the immune system including most, but not all leukemias and lymphomas *but this is not the most common result of infection with this virus.* The most common result of infection with FeLV is bone marrow and immune system suppression. Infected cats have profoundly low red and white blood cell counts and are very, very anemic. They develop chronic, repeated infections with bacteria and viruses that are normal, harmless inhabitants of the cat's body. When the immune system is suppressed by the feline leukemia virus, these otherwise innocuous germs cause diseases like chronic sinus infections and diarrhea. Other noncancerous consequences of infection include spinal cord problems and death in newborn kittens.

FeLV is transmitted from cat to cat in saliva through bite wounds, common use of food and water bowls, and mutual grooming; through urine by sharing litter boxes; and across the placenta from mother to offspring, and through the mammary gland in milk. One FeLV-infected cat can infect other members of a household or cattery; however, it could take several weeks of exposure before an infection occurs. Most cats are not exposed to enough virus to become infected.

When infection does occur, it begins in the tissues around the mouth and upper respiratory tract. Most cats develop antibodies against the virus that clear it from the system. In a small percentage of cats, protective antibodies will not be produced at the initial infection and these cats will become persistently infected. These cats will go on to develop one or more non-cancerous or cancerous FeLV-related diseases, usually within two years. Persistent infection with the feline leukemia virus is always fatal.

Although the viral infection itself is incurable, the virus-related diseases are treatable—even some of the cancers, giving the cat a good quality of life, albeit indefinite. However, because FeLV can be a complicating factor in any cat illness, it is important to test cats for the virus early on as part of the workup for *any serious organic, chronic, or recurrent disease.* Treatment early on during the course of an FeLV-related illness will improve the chances of response to that treatment.

There are a number of vaccines available to prevent persistent FeLV infection, however, none of the vaccines is 100 percent effective. The best prevention is by preventing exposure; keep your Maine coon cat indoors! Test any newly acquired cats before exposing them to the ones you already have. Don't allow stray cats to share food and water dishes with your cats. Isolate or remove FeLV-positive cats from your household and vaccinate all others. FeLV is not transmissible to humans.

Feline immunodeficiency virus (FIV) infection is associated with chronic respiratory and gastrointestinal infections, chronic and severe periodontal disease, and recurrent skin infections, all diseases that one might expect with a suppressed immune system. FIV has also been implicated in some neurologic and kidney diseases, and some cancers. It appears that the virus is transmitted between cats only by bite wounds, which is different from FeLV, which is transmitted through much more casual contact. The virus does not cross the placenta. Therefore, FIV is more difficult for cats to acquire.

Cats that are infected with FIV harbor the virus inside their bodies for several years before any disease consequences develop. Because the virus is difficult to transmit and because it can take many years for the cat to actually develop any disease, the significance of an infection is not fully understood. However, FIV-positive cats should be closely watched for illness, and treated early in the course of any disease. Isolation of a virus-positive cat is not necessary unless the cat is aggressive, in which case your pet could transmit the virus to others if they are bitten. There is no vaccine available for FIV at this time. Although this virus is classified similar to the human immunodeficiency virus, it is not transmissible to humans.

Feline infectious peritonitis (FIP) is also a viral infection. The virus infects the immune system cells called macrophages. These cells are found everywhere in the body: the liver, kidneys, eyes, brain and spinal cord, and uterus, and along the blood vessels along the walls of the chest and abdominal cavities. When these cells are invaded by the virus, the ensuing inflammation usually, but not always, causes a tremendous outpouring of fluid that fills the chest and abdomen. This fluid displaces organs and compresses the lungs making breathing difficult. Not surprisingly, some of the clinical signs of the infection include cyclic fever, depression and anorexia, labored breathing, and an enlarged abdomen. Weakness or paralysis and blindness are a consequence of the spinal cord, brain, and ocular inflammation. Pregnant cats may abort, or if the kittens are born live, they die soon afterward.

Cats become infected when they inhale or consume the virus shed in feces after using contaminated litter boxes or elimination areas. Not every cat who is carrying the virus in the gastrointestinal tract will become sick. Those that do become sick almost always die despite attempts at treatment. The virus is very hardy and can survive outside of the body in the environment for several weeks. A vaccine against FIP has been developed. Because it has only been in use for a short while, the safety and effectiveness of this vaccine is not known at this time. It should be used only on the advice of your veterinarian.

Rabies is a fatal viral disease of all warm-blooded animals including humans. In most cases of rabies, the virus is transmitted in the saliva of a rabid animal through a bite wound. After the virus enters the body, it travels along nerves to the brain and salivary glands. The virus causes seizures and dementia, respiratory failure, and death.

Important note: Rabies doesn't always cause furious dementia. Rabid animals can be depressed and comatose and as such are not likely to be recognized as being rabid. Humans and animals coming into contact with the saliva of these animals are at risk of contracting rabies.

Very important note: Cats have a tendency to develop the "dumb" form of rabies.

It can take from two weeks to six months or more from the time an animal is bitten until it is showing clinical signs of rabies. Although the animal can act perfectly normally during that time, it is able to transmit the virus to other animals if saliva gets on cuts or injured skin. To confirm the diagnosis of rabies, the animal must be euthanized and the brain examined for the virus.

Vaccinations are highly effective in preventing the disease even in the face of exposure. Currently in the United States, there have been more reported cases of rabies in cats than in dogs. All cats, even those that stay indoors, should be vaccinated against rabies at 12 weeks of age and again one year later. If there are no state or local laws governing rabies immunization, follow the manufacturer's recommendations for revaccination.

Miscellaneous Diseases

The Skin

Abscesses are painful pockets of pus under the skin. These pockets can be very soft and fluctuant to the touch, or very turgid. Abscesses are the result of puncture wounds, usually from the bite of another cat or other animal, that introduce bacteria, dirt, fur, and other contaminants from the environment into tissues. A puncture wound in your Maine coon cat's skin heals very quickly, but the bacteria and debris left behind cause infection and inflammation that result in the accumulation of pus and, thus, an abscess. After several uncomfortable days, the pressure of the abscess on the overlying skin may causes it to rupture, spilling forth a foul-smelling, thick, creamy, greenish yellow discharge. If the rupture is small, it will heal over quickly and the abscess will reform and become larger.

Important note: Proper treatment for abscess includes establishing good drainage so that the underlying tissues heal at the same time as the skin wounds. This may involve surgery to remove damaged tissue and skin and placement of one or more drains to allow the pus to continue to discharge for several days. Warm compresses and possibly flushing the area with an antiseptic solution aid in this process. Owners should wear gloves and avoid contact with the discharge. Bacteria in pus can contaminate cuts in the skin and result in infection. Antibiotics are of secondary importance to drainage in effective treatment of abscesses.

Important note: If you live in a rabies endemic area, your Maine coon cat should be given a booster inoculation for rabies after such a bite for both your pet's and your protection.

Miliary dermatitis is the generic term for a condition recognized by the appearance of crusts and scabs scattered over the cat's body from the head to the base of the tail. This is a hypersensitivity or allergic reaction, usually the result of an allergy to fleas. Other potential causes include food hypersensitivity, ringworm infection, pollen or other inhalant allergies, or bacterial dermatitis. Treatment includes avoiding exposure to the allergic substance and judicious use of corticosteroids if appropriate.

Important note: Because 99 percent of the time this condition is due to exposure to fleas, flea control is imperative to diagnosis and treatment. Once adequate flea control is ensured, other diagnostic tests and therapeutic trials are advised.

Ringworm is a fungal disease of the skin and hair follicle. Kittens and cats are exposed to the fungus in the environment and through contact with infected cats that shed the fungus in the fur. Not every infected cat will show the characteristic scaly patches of hair loss, usually on the head and limbs and occasionally on the body. Some cats harbor the fungus without any clinical signs. A diagnosis of ringworm is made by demonstrating the growth of the fungus in the hair shafts or by culturing it on special growth media in the laboratory. Treatment varies from topical anti-fungal creams, shampoos, or dips, and oral medications, depending upon the severity of the condition and the number of cats in a household that carry the fungus. A recently licensed ringworm vaccine may help control the spread of ringworm in a cattery or colony.

Important note: Ringworm is communicable to other pets and humans, especially children and immunosuppressed individuals. All symptomatic cats should be treated and an attempt should be made to decontaminate the environment by vacuuming to remove the cat hair and dander and washing surfaces with diluted bleach solutions when possible.

The Circulatory and Respiratory Systems

Cardiomyopathy is a disease of the heart's muscle. There are several types of cardiomyopathy in cats, but most cases occur in one of two forms: dilated or hypertrophic. Cardiomyopathy can occur as a disease all by itself, or it can occur secondary to other illness. Hypertrophic cardiomyopathy may be an inherited disease in Maine coons and other breeds. Although both forms of cardiomyopathy result in separate and distinct types of damage to the heart muscle, the end result is the same, i.e., heart failure. This heart failure usually progresses slowly over weeks to months or even years. In fact, you may not even be aware that your Maine coon cat is sick until the heart has been severely damaged. Signs of cardiomyopathy include difficulty in breathing, weakness, coughing, loss of appetite, severe pain or loss of control of the rear legs, or sudden death. Treatment for cardiomyopathy includes eliminating the underlying cause if possible, along with medication to improve the function of the heart.

Important note: Dilated cardiomyopathy is often a nutritionally related disease caused by a dietary deficiency of the amino acid taurine. Although most cat food manufacturers supplement their foods with adequate amounts of this nutrient, occasionally a cat will have a greater nutritional requirement than is provided in commercial diets. Cats eating inexpensive, poorly formulated diets, home-cooked diets, or vegetarian or exclusively organ meat diets are also at risk for developing dilated cardiomyopathy. Feeding your Maine coon cat a well-known and respected brand of commercial cat food is the best way to prevent nutritionally related dilated cardiomyopathy.

Important note: A form of hypertrophic cardiomyopathy is often a secondary disease associated with hyperthyroidism in geriatric cats. It is reversible with treatment of hyperthyroidism. Annual physical examination of your Maine coon cat, especially in its older years, is very important.

Respiratory infections are usually caused by any one of a number of viruses endemic and easily transmissible in the cat population. These viruses live within the respiratory passages of healthy appearing cats that periodically shed the virus into the environment. These cats are called asymptomatic carriers. Unvaccinated or immunosuppressed cats coming in contact with these viruses develop upper respiratory infections characterized by sneezing and watery discharge from the eyes and nose. Viral infections damage the mucous membranes of the respiratory passages and allow bacteria to multiply. The watery ocular and nasal discharge changes to a mucus or pus consistency. Occasionally the infection is spread to lower respiratory tissues resulting in pneumonia. More often, repeated or long-standing infections damage the defense mechanisms in the nasal, sinus, and respiratory passages causing chronic or repeated and often incurable upper respiratory signs.

Important note: To prevent chronic respiratory infections in your Maine coon cat, follow these steps:
1. Purchase kittens from reputable and disease-free sources only. Question your sources about infections within their cattery, home, or pet store and be alert for signs of respiratory disease when you visit these places.
2. Have your new kitten vaccinated for the common respiratory viruses

Watery eyes and a runny nose are signs of an upper respiratory infection, just as they are in humans.

and keep current on yearly vaccinations.
3. Have new kittens examined by a veterinarian prior to introduction into your home with other cats.
4. Isolate new arrivals for two weeks if you have any suspicions about respiratory disease in the new additions.
5. If you are a multi-Maine coon cat household and have an outbreak, consult a veterinarian familiar with the special requirements for disease control in catteries.

The Eyes and Ears

Conjunctivitis is an inflammation of the delicate tissues around the eye and occurs alone or in conjunction with upper respiratory infections. Signs include blinking and rubbing of the eyes, redness, swelling, and a discharge that can be thin and watery or thick and cloudy. Like infections of the respiratory system, conjunctivitis can be caused by viruses, but bacteria, irritant vapors such as smoke or chemicals, and blunt trauma to the eye can cause conjunctivitis too.

Important note: Some of these signs also occur with more serious diseases. Conjunctivitis can also

HOW-TO:
Basic Nursing Care

Take Your Maine Coon Cat's Temperature

Use a standard rectal thermometer to check your Maine coon cat's temperature. Either an inexpensive glass and mercury type costing about $2 or a digital readout model ranging in price from $3 to $15 works fine. If you use a glass thermometer, shake it until the mercury reads below 96°F (35.6°C). Follow the manufacturer's instructions on how to reset the digital version. Lubricate the tip with petrolatum or use a pre-lubricated disposable sheath to make insertion more comfortable for your cat. It's best to have all these preparations done ahead of time before you enlist your cat into this endeavor. Place your cat on a waist-high surface such as a countertop or vanity table so that you have more control over the procedure. If your cat is

really not feeling well, it may be very cooperative and put up little resistance. If your pet struggles aggressively, have an assistant hold the cat by the scruff of its neck and/or stretch it on its side so that you can insert the thermometer into its rectum. Make the insertion approximately parallel to its backbone. Insert a glass thermometer at least half its length and insert the entire length of the probe of a digital thermometer. If resistance is encountered, try turning the thermometer or redirecting it slightly to avoid fecal material in the rectum. Leave the thermometer in place for two minutes or until the digital one signals that the reading is complete.

The normal body temperature for your Maine coon cat is 100.5 to 102.5°F (38–39.2°C). It may register a little higher if your cat is very agitated about having the thermometer inserted. Elevated body temperature in a reasonably calm cat suggests a fever. A low temperature reading means that the thermometer

was not inserted long enough or far enough into the rectum; was inserted into fecal material which can lead to inaccurate readings; or is a defective instrument. It could mean that your cat is gravely ill and you should contact your veterinarian as soon as possible. Low body temperatures are often detected in young kittens as they cannot regulate their body temperature until about two or three weeks of age. A kitten's body temperature must be over 96°F (35.6°C) in order to digest milk from its mother or from a bottle.

Give Your Maine Coon Cat Oral Medication

Have your medicine ready—either the pill or capsule out of the bottle or the liquid drawn into the dropper—before you go to get your cat. Place your cat on a waist-high surface with its back end against you. Using one hand, hold your cat's head on both sides of its cheekbones. With the other hand, hold the medication with your thumb and finger and pry open your pet's mouth by pushing down on its lower jaw. Drop the medication as far back into your cat's mouth as you can. If your cat is cooperative, you may be able to push the tablet or capsule with your finger over the back of its tongue before you release its head. Close its mouth and stroke under the chin until you see your cat swallow. It's always a good idea to open your cat's mouth again to see if the pill is gone because some cats are remarkably good at hiding them. If you're not comfortable about putting your fingers in or near your Maine

To give your pet oral medication, secure its head with one hand while holding the medication and at the same time prying open the mouth with your other hand. Drop or push the medication as far back on the cat's tongue as you can . . . then close your pet's mouth and stroke under the chin until you are sure the medication has been swallowed.

coon cat's mouth, a "piller" is a useful device to do this for you. Purchase one from a pet store or your veterinarian.

For liquid medications, again place your cat on a waist-high surface. Grasp its head as you would to give a pill. Insert the medicine dropper between its teeth on the side of its mouth and administer the medication in one or more squirts over its tongue. If your cat should spit or drool out more medication than it swallows, consult your veterinarian about changing to a pill or capsule form of the drug to insure more accurate dosing.

Instill Ear Ointments and Drops

Examine the inside of the ear or pinna for the opening of the ear canal. The opening will be obscured by arcs and folds of skin-covered cartilage and a tuft of hair. This opening is the entrance to an L-shaped canal. The eardrum or tympanic membrane at its base is not visible without an otoscope. To instill medicated ointment or drops effectively, you must place the drops into the opening, not on the pinna. Hold the pinna and release the drops as close to the ear canal opening as possible. If you are using an ointment, insert the tip of the tube directly into the canal and squeeze in the desired amount of medication. Continue to hold on to the pinna while you gently massage below the ear. This will promote the flow of medication into the lower horizontal portion of the canal toward the tympanic membrane.

To administer ear drops, have an assistant hold your pet steady while you secure its head with one hand and instill the ear drops with the other hand. Make sure the drops go into the opening of the ear canal, which is inside the ear and obscured by cartilage and hair.

Instill Eye Ointments and Drops

Your Maine coon cat has three eyelids on each eye: the two furry ones that blink at you and a third fleshy lid located below the other two. You can see it in the inner corner of its eye as a wedge-shaped flap. This third lid is called a nictitating membrane and it helps to sweep the eye clean of debris and distribute the tears. Your Maine coon cat can pull the nictitating membrane partially over the eye to protect it at will.

You will need help to instill eye medication in your pet. Have your assistant hold your pet's head steady while rolling down the lower lid to form a small pocket into which you can squeeze or drop the medication. If using ointment, open and close the lids to distribute the medication. Eye drops will be distributed over the eye automatically.

Sometimes this lid comes up if a cat isn't feeling well.

To instill medicated eye ointment or drops, roll the lower lid down to create a small pocket. Squeeze about a 0.25-inch (3 millimeter) strip of ointment into the pocket, then open and close the lids to distribute the medication over the eye. For eyedrops, simply instill the desired number of drops into the pocket; it isn't necessary to open and close the lids in this case. Try not to touch the tip of the tube or bottle to anything.

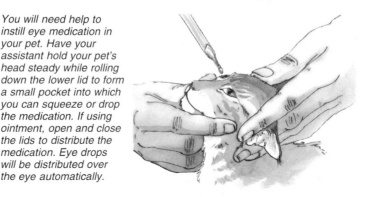

become chronic and refractory to treatment. For these reasons, have your veterinarian examine your Maine coon cat if it exhibits any ocular problems.

Ear mites are insect parasites whose relatives include free-living mites and mites that cause mange in a variety of animals. Ear mites prefer to live in the ear canals of cats and dogs (they're not particularly selective about either of the two) but they can also be found in the fur. Ear mites are easily transmitted from animal to animal, but kittens seem to be the most susceptible to infestation. Cats and kittens with ear mites have intensely itchy ears, and the canals are occluded by a dark, waxy debris that looks like coffee grounds.

Important note: It is decidedly easier now, more so than in the past, to treat ear mites by using any one of a number of highly effective *prescription* topical, oral, or injectable medications. However, all the cats and the dogs in the household must be treated for ear mites at the same time, whether or not they are showing signs of infestation, or the infestation will remain in your pet population. A resistance to heavy reinfestation may or may not develop once a kitten or cat is cleared of the mites. Your Maine coon cat can be reinfested if it comes in contact with other animals carrying the mites. Ear mites do not infect people.

Otitis, or inflammation of the ear, should be suspected if your Maine coon cat shakes and scratches its head excessively, sneezes and has noisy breathing, has an odor or discharge from its ears, tilts its head persistently to one side, has pupils of unequal size in uniform light, abnormal eye movements, problems with balance, and, of course, apparent deafness. Otitis is usually the result of a bacterial, yeast, or parasitic infection in the ear canal or deeper structures, but tumors and trauma to the head can also cause these signs.

Important note: A common assumption held by many cat owners is that a cat has ear mites when it is bothered by its ears. The owners then simply use an over-the-counter or home remedy for ear mites rather than seek examination and diagnosis by a veterinarian. More often than not, this delays proper treatment and causes unnecessary suffering for the cat.

The Digestive System

Constipation is the result of an inability to pass feces due to an obstruction (fractured pelvis, intestinal tumor), loss of nerve function to the colon or rectum (seen with trauma to the pelvis, aging), inadequate fiber in the diet, excessive water loss (dehydration due to illness or diuretics), inaccessible litter area (litter box not available, broken bones that make it difficult for the cat to get around), and behavior problems. Constipated cats may or may not strain to pass feces; a few cats make no attempt at all to defecate. Depending upon the cause, constipation can be transient, occasional, or an ongoing problem. Treatment includes manipulation of the diet, laxatives, and medications to promote forward movement of feces. Surgery is occasionally advisable.

Important note: Severe, chronic constipation may require multiple enemas or anesthesia and manual removal of the impacted feces. Effective treatment for this type of constipation requires that the owner be aware of the cat's elimination habits in order to minimize the need for this kind of intervention.

Hair balls are matlike accumulations of hair in the stomach of your cat. The hair accumulates after grooming and consuming small fur-bearing prey such as mice. In this case, the hair is likely to also contain small pieces of the skeleton. Hair balls develop because a cat's stomach does not empty in between meals and they have a very small pylorus, or outflow, opening to their stomach. Small hair balls pass through, large hair balls must come up and out. All cats can have hair balls, but long-haired cats like your Maine coon cat are likely to have them with more frequency. Daily combing will minimize hair ball formation. Flavored petrolatum-based laxatives and added fiber in the diet can be useful in chronic cases.

Important note: Vomiting an occasional hair ball is not to be of concern, but chronic vomiting due to hair balls can cause anatomic problems in the stomach. If you are finding evidence that your Maine coon cat is vomiting hair balls containing remnants of its prey, your pet should be dewormed for intestinal parasites regularly. Do not assume that all vomiting is due to hair balls, especially if the vomiting is persistent and/or if you do not actually find hair in the vomitus. In this case, consult your veterinarian.

Common intestinal parasites that are seen in kittens and cats include a number of worms and primitive organisms called protozoa. All of these parasites have the potential to cause disease by obstructing the intestinal tract, inciting inflammation as they migrate through tissues, or robbing your Maine coon cat of nutrients. Kittens and adult cats that are sick from other illnesses are the most susceptible to the consequences of intestinal parasite infections. Healthy cats often harbor intestinal parasites without any apparent detrimental effects. (See Intestinal Parasite Control, page 86.)

Important note: Some of these parasites have the potential, in one form or another, to infect humans or other animals. Although the parasite may be "well-adapted" and cause minimal disease in healthy adult cats, human infection can be devastating. If your Maine coon cat goes outdoors, have its feces examined for parasites at least once a year.

Diseases of the liver are not rare in cats and in many cases neither the inciting cause nor the predisposing factors to explain why some cats get liver disease are often determined, although bacterial and viral infections and exposure to toxins are often suspected. One specific virus, feline infectious peritonitis virus, is a known cause of liver disease. Periods of anorexia in overweight cats is one well-documented predisposing factor. Liver disease is often a chronic disease with an insidious onset. Except for possibly jaundice, there are few clinical signs that point in the way of liver disease on physical examination. These cats have nonspecific sick cat signs: vomiting, weight loss, depression, and loss of appetite. The diagnosis may be suspected on a physical examination but usually requires laboratory analysis of blood and other diagnostic tests including a liver biopsy to confirm those suspicions. Many cases of liver disease are treatable based on the results of such testing.

Important note: Because of the association of liver disease with lack of food intake, your Maine coon cat should not be allowed to go longer than 48 hours without food, especially if it is obese. Such a period of anorexia warrants an examination by your veterinarian.

Vomiting and diarrhea are common clinical signs of disease in several body systems, but most often occur as a result of some disruption of the normal function of the stomach or intestines. Vomiting and diarrhea can occur alone or together due to a number of causes. Some vomiting seems almost normal in cats. Your Maine coon cat will vomit to eliminate hair (see Hair balls, page 98) that accumulates in its stomach while grooming, and undigestible remnants of the carcasses of its prey that are too large to pass into its intestinal tract. Switching from brand to brand or flavor to flavor of cat food may cause vomiting (or diarrhea) in your cat, by disrupting the normal "ecology" of the bacteria in the gastrointestinal system. Infectious agents such as intestinal parasites, bacteria, or viruses cause these signs in any cat, especially the young.

Important note: Most cases of vomiting and diarrhea resolve on their own without any treatment. Your Maine coon cat will act fairly normally but may not eat much, if at all, for a day or so. However, minor episodes of vomiting and diarrhea that initially appear to be of little consequence can in fact worsen over time, or be clinical signs of more serious gastrointestinal or systemic disease. If vomiting worsens or persists, especially in young kittens, seek veterinary assistance.

My tip: Always bring a sample of your Maine coon cat's feces with you, even if your cat stays indoors.

The Urinary System

Feline urologic syndrome (FUS) is a specific clinical syndrome related to the formation of mineral crystals in the urine and is the most commonly occurring disorder in a list of diseases of the lower urinary tract in all cats including Maine coon cats. Because this syndrome is uncomfortable and even painful, affected cats strain to urinate, urinate in inappropriate locations around the house, and pass small amounts of urine frequently. The urine may contain blood and if so will range from slightly pink to port wine in color. Your Maine coon cat may groom his prepuce or her vulva exces-

sively due to the discomfort. Although this syndrome occurs in both male and female cats, the urethra may become obstructed by the crystals in male cats, resulting in acute and fatal kidney failure.

Researchers have attempted to pin a cause on FUS for many years. Some of these suggested causes include bacterial and viral infections, and early neutering. The only consistent association between FUS and its occurrence is the cat's diet. Affected cats are almost always eating a kibble-type diet too high in magnesium or one that causes the cat's urine to become alkaline after meals. In the initial treatment, cats with FUS are placed on a diet that promotes the dissolution of the crystals and allows the bladder to heal. If a urinary catheter has been passed to relieve an obstruction, antibiotics are almost always used to prevent a *secondary* infection with bacteria that may have been introduced into the bladder. Once the initial episode of FUS has been controlled, a maintenance diet is used to prevent recurrence.

Important note: Primary bacterial infections are present in only about 2 percent of all cases of FUS. Antibiotics alone are not effective in the treatment of FUS; therapy must include lifelong dietary management to eliminate the inflammation and prevent recurrence.

Important note: Recurrence is almost guaranteed to happen unless your Maine coon cat eats a diet with carefully controlled magnesium levels and formulated to produce an acidic urine. No cheating! There are several available. Follow your veterinarian's recommendations.

Important note: Not all cases of dysuria (difficulty in urinating) are related to FUS. True urinary tract infections, malformations of the genito-urinary system, tumors, neurologic diseases, endocrine diseases, and trauma can also cause these signs. Your veterinarian will recommend certain diagnostic testing based on the specific history and findings in each case.

Diseases of the kidney can occur in any age of cat; however, kidney disease is usually seen in middle-aged to older cats and, in fact, is the most common cause of nontraumatic death in geriatric cats. The term kidney or renal disease is a general one that is applied to any dysfunction of this organ from a number of causes. Because the kidneys act as filters, they are easily damaged by poisons and are an ideal location for bacterial and viral infections to settle in. Although the kidneys are well protected by their location within the abdominal cavity, they may be damaged through trauma. Cat foods that are highly acidified and low in potassium have been linked to kidney disease. Most causes of kidney disease, however, are never known.

Like the liver, kidneys have a tremendous reserve capacity. Nearly 75 percent of the kidneys must be damaged before your Maine coon cat will begin to show any signs that they are not functioning adequately. With a 75 percent loss in kidney function, clinical signs of poor appetite, weight loss, vomiting, increased water consumption, and volume of urine produced begin to appear.

Important note: Even with severe renal disease, your Maine coon cat may show few if any of the signs listed above, and those signs may be quite mild or intermittent. An annual physical examination by your veterinarian and careful observation by you are the best insurance for early detection of kidney disease.

Renal diseases are treated by taking steps to support the remaining kidney function and to correct the effects of kidney disease on other systems in the body. This includes fluid therapy, and anti-emetic and anti-ulcer drugs to control vomiting and gastritis. Low-phosphorus and low-protein diets are used to control the imbalance of calcium and phosphorus in the blood, which is a serious consequence of renal disease. Oral potassium supplements may be used. Another important complication of renal disease is anemia. Some cats are given the hormone erythropoietin to stimulate their bone marrow to produce red blood cells and correct the anemia.

Important note: The prognosis for kidney disease is variable and depends on several factors: the cause, if known, and if it can be eliminated, the age of the cat, the amount of healthy kidney tissue that remains, and other organ systems that may be affected. One of the best prognostic indicators for cats with kidney disease is their appetite. If they continue to eat, the prognosis is much better than if they do not.

The Endocrine System

Hyperthyroidism is a common endocrine disease being recognized with increasing frequency as cats live longer and longer lives. Hyperthyroidism is a condition caused by excessive blood levels of the hormone called thyroxine. This hormone is produced by two glands located in the neck. With age, these glands can become enlarged and even develop tumors (usually benign), and begin to produce thyroxine in amounts that exceed the body's needs. The excess thyroxine has a number of effects on several body systems, including the cardiovascular system, to cause heart disease. Hyperthyroid cats are often ravenously hungry, but despite a huge intake of food, they lose weight. Hyperthyroid cats often have intermittent vomiting and/or diarrhea and may

Intestinal Parasites of Cats

Parasite	Mode(s) of transmission	Clinical signs of disease	Diagnosis	Treatment
Roundworms	Ingestion of eggs passed in feces; larvae cross the placenta and mammary glands in milk.	Potbelly, poor hair coat, malnutrition in kittens; vomiting or diarrhea; may be asymptomatic in adults.	Eggs found on fecal flotation tests; worms found in feces or vomitus.	Various medications to kill the intestinal worms; remove feces from environment.
Hookworms	Ingestion of larvae that hatch from eggs passed in feces.	Diarrhea; weight loss.	Eggs found on fecal flotation test.	Same as roundworms.
Whipworms	Ingestion of larvae that hatch from eggs passed in feces.	Diarrhea; weight loss.	Same as hookworms.	Same as hookworms.
Dipylidium tapeworms	Ingestion of fleas containing the tapeworm eggs.	Infestation is usually not a problem in otherwise healthy cats.	Ricelike segments found on the fur around the anus and perineum.	Medication to eliminate the intestinal worms; flea control to prevent infestation.
Taenia tapeworms	Ingestion of infective cysts in the tissues of small prey.	Rarely, passage of tapeworms in the feces; many infections are asymptomatic.	Tapeworm eggs on fecal flotation test.	Medication to kill intestinal worms; discourage hunting and consuming prey.
Coccidia	Ingestion of cysts.	Diarrhea; blood in feces.	Cysts found on fecal flotation test.	Antibiotics.
Toxoplasma	Ingestion of infective oocysts or tissue cysts in small prey; tissue forms cross the placenta and infect kittens before birth.	Diarrhea, eye problems, neurologic problems; most infections go unnoticed.	A definitive diagnosis of true toxoplasmosis is very difficult. Occasionally oocysts can be found on fecal flotation tests in cats with diarrhea; serologic tests may be helpful in other forms of the disease.	Antibiotics.

drink a lot of water. Hyperthyroidism is diagnosed by measuring the thyroxine level in the blood. Treatment for hyperthyroidism includes medication, surgery, and radiation therapy. There are pros and cons for all three.

Important note: As most hyperthyroid cats are old at the time of diagnosis, a thorough health screen for other diseases is important when considering treatment. However, advanced age is not a reason to withhold treatment, even surgery, in an otherwise healthy geriatric cat.

Affecting More Than One Body System

Cancer is an unregulated growth of cells in any organ of the body. This unregulated grow is divided into two kinds: malignant growth, which spreads from the primary site to other locations by way of the circulatory system (blood and lymphatic), and benign growth, which does not spread. Benign tumors are generally regarded as less serious because they can usually be surgically removed in their entirety. This is not always the case; some benign neoplasms are highly invasive into the area where they arise, making complete excision impossible. Both malignant and benign tumors disrupt or obliterate the architecture and function of normal tissues around them. The gastrointestinal, circulatory, and immune systems, and skin are common locations for cancers in cats.

Cancer can occur in any age of cat but is usually seen in older ones. With good nutrition and preventative health care, your Maine coon cat can easily live to the age of 15 or older, making the possibility of developing cancer significant. The clinical signs of cancer will depend upon the location from which it arises. Signs may be nonexistent until late in the course of the disease in slowly developing cancers, or

sudden and severe in aggressive cases. The definitive diagnosis of cancer in any location is of course biopsy.

Surgery is still the treatment of choice for most cancers, especially those of the skin and gastrointestinal system, however both radiation and chemotherapy are useful for some tumors. As in other geriatric diseases of cats, age alone should not be used to decide whether or not to treat your Maine coon cat for cancer. The overall health and quality of life of your pet must be taken into consideration.

Important note: *Cancer is not always fatal.* Treatment, especially surgical, is curative in many cases. Even palliative treatment can provide a good quality of life for a period of time. Ask your veterinarian for a referral to a veterinary oncologist if you have questions about your options.

Food intolerance/allergies are not uncommon and may affect your Maine coon cat through two body systems: the skin and/or gastrointestinal systems. When affecting the skin, food intolerances or allergies cause intense itching, usually around the face and neck. Sores and hair loss result from the cat's scratching. Sometimes the sores and hair loss will be extensive and include the whole body. Corticosteroid drugs traditionally used to control itching in allergic reactions are generally of limited benefit for the pruritus associated with food intolerance. Food intolerance or allergies that affect the gastrointestinal system can also cause vomiting and/or diarrhea. Vomiting may be almost immediate or may occur several hours after eating. Diarrhea may contain blood.

Your Maine coon cat can develop a food intolerance to major food ingredients, such as beef or eggs, or to minor food ingredients, such as the added artificial colorings or preservatives. Food intolerance is diagnosed most accurately by feeding a carefully controlled, limited, home-cooked diet for several weeks. Once the offending food substance(s) is identified, a balanced hypoallergenic commercial diet is slowly substituted for the home-cooked one.

Important note: It may take several trials before the appropriate diet is found, which can be discouraging. Some cases require medication, too.

Important note: Most cases of the itchies in cats are due to flea infestation. Before you embark on a long, possibly labor intensive food trial, be sure that your flea control is absolutely stellar.

Considering Euthanasia

The act of euthanasia is a great gift. With it, pet owners can give their pets freedom from pain and misery. Because one of the things I am often asked as a veterinarian is to put patients to sleep, I try to focus on this "good." Without some type of coping strategy, it can be overwhelming when the act of euthanasia brings an end to years of human-animal devotion.

The two worst things about euthanasia are making the decision to end your pet's life and coping with living without your cat. Just because the capability now exists to deal with many medical and aging problems, it doesn't mean one should. Sometimes life's circumstances indicate that one should not. The decision is a personal one that must be made within the family and with the guidance of the veterinarian. Once the decision to euthanize a pet is made, the owner almost always feels relief. Open grieving is important for coping with the loss of an important companion. Grief counseling is available and encouraged. It's not "just a cat."

Regular health checks and vaccinations will ensure a healthy, happy Maine coon for many, many years.

The process of euthanasia is simple. Your veterinarian will administer an injection of a drug that acts as a potent anesthetic. The drug first makes the animal unconscious of pain and other stimuli, usually within a few seconds. Then it causes both breathing and the heart to stop. This takes about a minute. The injection is made into a vein using a needle or an intravenous catheter. In animals with very low blood pressure, it may be necessary to inject the drug directly into the heart.

Euthanasia is painless except for the prick of the needle or catheter as it enters the skin. If an animal is very apprehensive, a sedative can be administered prior to this process. If you wish to be with your cat at the time of euthanasia, tell your veterinarian. Some people do, some do not. You should also ask to be left alone with your cat before and after euthanasia if you wish. It's a good idea to make all these decisions ahead of time, including arrangements to pay or be billed for any charges. Even if you think you will be very strong, many people become emotional at the time of their pet's death. Consider asking a friend or family member to be with you. Some veterinarians will perform euthanasia at home.

After an animal is euthanized, provisions must be made for the body. It is routine for several bodies to be cremated at the same time and the ashes disposed of through a commercial provider. Some people prefer private cremation and to have the ashes returned. Most veterinarians can accommodate this preference, but there will be an additional fee. You may also wish to bury the body at home. A very good book to help young children cope with the death of a cat is *The Tenth Good Thing About Barney,* by Judith Viorst (see Books, page 108).

Glossary

anemia a condition of having inadequate numbers of red blood cells in circulation

antibodies chemicals made by immune system cells called lymphocytes in response to bacteria and other foreign substances that enter the body. Antibodies combine with bacteria and assist in destroying and removing them from the body. Vaccines mimic the properties of bacteria that stimulate the lymphocytes. Antibodies are transferred to newborns via the colostrum or "first milk" to provide protection against infectious diseases until the newborn's own immune system is well-enough developed to make antibodies on its own.

calorie a unit of heat that is released when a food is burned by the body for fuel

classic a tabby marking pattern consisting of dense, dark markings in a whorl or butterfly pattern along the sides; also called "blotched"

cornea the clear covering of the eye through which light passes

dam the mother

diuretics drugs and chemicals that promote water loss from the body and associated increase in urination

dystocia difficulty with labor and delivery of offspring

dysuria difficulty urinating

elimination urination or defection

endocrine involving the hormone-producing organs and glands

external genitalia the sexual organs consisting of the vulva and associated structures in females, and the scrotum and prepuce in males

feline acne a skin disorder where pustules and blackheads occur on the chin

feral wild, especially an animal that is normally considered domesticated

feti the term for unborn kittens (and other animals) during the second and third trimester of pregnancy

flea dirt the waste product excreted by the flea after consuming the blood of the host animal; flea feces

flooding a behavior modification technique where the subject (animal or human) is continuously exposed to a stimulus until it no longer reacts

germicidal lethal to bacteria, viruses, and other organisms of disease

gestation pregnancy

health certificate a document obtained from a veterinarian that verifies that an animal is in good health for travel

hepatic lipidosis a liver disease of cats associated with anorexia resulting in the accumulation of fat within the liver and destruction of its normal structure and function

heritable transferred from parent to offspring through genes

house soiling urinating and defecating in inappropriate locations around the house

immunosuppression a state of decreased ability to fight infection from bacteria and other germs

inoculation a vaccination or immunization against infectious disease

insect growth regulator (IGR) a group of laboratory-made insect hormones that render female fleas sterile by a number of different mechanisms

jowls the prominent fleshy cheeks that develop in breeding tom cats

mackerel a tabby marking pattern consisting of narrow bands of vertical stripes on the body

neurologic involving the brain, spinal column, and nerves

nutrients chemical substances provided in the diet or made by the body that fuel and energize physiologic processes and serve as precursors for structural components of the body

obligate required

otoscope the instrument used to examine the ear canal and drum

perineum the area of skin surrounding the anus and vulva in the female or the anus, scrotum, and prepuce in the male

periodontal disease painful infection and inflammation of the gums and the ligaments that hold the teeth into the jaw, often associated with cavities and fractured teeth

plaque the slime of bacteria and their waste products on the teeth

prepuce the reflection of skin covering the penis, roughly equivalent to the human foreskin

pride a social group of lions

pruritus itching

psittacines a large group of hook-billed birds that includes parrots and macaws

pupa the final stage in the flea life cycle from which emerges the adult, reproducing flea. Pupae are highly resistant to pesticides and cold temperatures and allow fleas to "overwinter"

pyrethrins a group of pesticides derived from a species of chrysanthemum that possess a quick-kill effect on fleas and other insects

scrotal sac the pouch between the anus and prepuce that contains the testicles

tartar the deposit formed from the mineralization and hardening of plaque on the teeth

trimester one third of gestation or pregnancy

ultrasound a diagnostic technique that uses high-frequency sound waves to identify anatomical structures

urethra the anatomic connection between the urinary bladder and the outside

virulent powerful, strong, or highly potent and capable of producing disease.

Useful Addresses and Literature

Associations

Maine Coon Breeders and
  Fanciers' Association (MCBFA)
  c/o Deborah Frick
  4405 Karrol S.W.
  Albuquerque, NM 87121

The American Cat Association
  (ACA)
  8101 Katherine Avenue
  Panorama City, CA 91402
  (818) 782-6080

American Cat Fanciers
  Association (ACFA)
  P.O. Box 203
  Point Lookout, MO 65726
  (417) 334-5430

The Cat Fanciers' Association,
  Inc. (CFA)
  1805 Atlantic Avenue
  P.O. Box 1005
  Manasquan, NJ 08736
  (908) 528-9797

The International Cat
  Association (TICA)
  P.O. Box 2684
  Harlingen, TX 78551
  (210) 428-8046

National Animal Poison
  Control Center
  College of Veterinary Medicine
  University of Illinois
  Urbana, IL 61801
  1-800-548-2423; have a
  credit card available; consul-
  tation fee is $30 per case

with free follow-up calls, or
call: 1-900-680-0000; fee is
$20 for first five minutes,
$2.95 per minute thereafter.

Books

Behrend, K. and M. Wegler.
  *The Complete Book of Cat
  Care: How to Raise a Happy
  and Healthy Cat.* Hauppauge,
  New York: Barron's
  Educational Series, Inc.,
  1991.

Daly, Carol Himsel. *Caring For
  Your Sick Cat.* Hauppauge,
  New York: Barron's
  Educational Series, Inc.,
  1994.

Frye, Fredric L. *First Aid for
  Your Cat.* Hauppauge, New
  York: Barron's Educational
  Series, Inc., 1987.

Hornidge, Marilis. *That Yankee
  Cat.* revised edition. Tilbury
  House, Publishers, Gardiner,
  1991.

Maggitti, Phil. *Guide to a Well-
  Behaved Cat.* Hauppauge,
  New York: Barron's
  Educational Series, Inc.,
  1993.

Viorst, Judith. *The Tenth Good
  Thing About Barney.* New
  York: Simon and Schuster,
  1987.

Magazines and Other Publications

CAT FANCY Magazine,
  published monthly by
  Fancy Publications, Inc.
  3 Burroughs
  Irvine, CA 92718.
  Subscription: $25.97 for
  12 issues; single issues:
  $2.95 at newsstands.

CATS Magazine, published
  monthly by
  CATS Magazine, Inc.
  2750-A South Ridgewood
  Avenue
  South Daytona, FL 32119
  Subscription: $21.97
  ($25.97 for Exhibitors Edition)
  for one year, single issues:
  $2.50 at newsstands.

Available from the MCBFA:
  *Caring For, Breeding and
  Showing Your Maine Coon
  Cat* ($7, includes shipping
  and handling) and *Genetics
  for the Maine Coon Cat
  Breeder*, by Amanda Thomas
  ($5, includes shipping and
  handling). To order, contact
  Trish Simpson, Editor,
  13283 Deron Avenue
  San Diego, CA 92129.

Index